The Complete

Mediterranean Cookbook:

150 Quick & Healthy Recipes for Busy Beginners

+ 30-Day Meal Plan

Introduction

Dear Readers,

Welcome to the *Mediterranean Diet Cookbook!* I'm thrilled that you've chosen to embark on this journey with me to explore the Mediterranean's flavors, health benefits, and vibrant lifestyle.

The Mediterranean Diet is not just a way of eating; it's a lifestyle rooted in centuries of tradition, culture, and health. Originating from the countries bordering the Mediterranean Sea, such as Greece, Italy, Spain, and southern France, this diet emphasizes fresh, wholesome ingredients that nourish the body and soul. Rich in fruits, vegetables, whole grains, healthy fats, and lean proteins, the Mediterranean Diet has been hailed for its ability to promote heart health, reduce the risk of chronic diseases, and foster longevity.

The Mediterranean Diet has long been celebrated for its delicious, fresh ingredients and its ability to nourish the body and mind. For me, it's more than just a diet — it's a way of living that embraces balance, mindfulness, and joy in everyday meals. This cookbook reflects that philosophy, designed to inspire you to eat well, feel great, and enjoy the process of cooking wholesome food.

Whether you're new to the Mediterranean Diet or a long-time enthusiast, my goal with this collection is to offer something for everyone. The recipes are simple yet full of flavor, encouraging you to use seasonal, natural ingredients that are good for you and the planet. From fresh salads and hearty main dishes to delightful desserts, I hope you'll discover how easy and rewarding it can be to make Mediterranean cooking a part of your everyday routine.

Thank you for allowing me to share this experience with you. I hope these recipes bring as much joy to your kitchen as they have to mine. Welcome to the Mediterranean lifestyle — where food is medicine, and every meal celebrates life!

With gratitude and excitement,
Joanne Hauser

Table of Contents

BREAKFAST

LUNCHES

SALADS

DINNER

SMOOTHIE

DESSERTS

The main principles of the diet. List of foods

9

The main principles of the diet. List of foods

The diet consists of 60% carbohydrates, 10% proteins, and 30% fats. However, the fats and carbohydrates chosen for a weight loss plan must be the suitable types. This includes whole wheat pasta, legumes, and different varieties of whole grain bread. Also, incorporate olive oil, avocado, and fatty fish. Adding a fresh vegetable salad and greens, creates a healthy lunch option.

This system does not impose strict limitations or specific methods. Instead, it categorizes foods into three groups:

• Foods to be included in the daily diet;
• Foods to be consumed 1-4 times a week;
• Foods permitted up to 1-2 times a month.

Greens...

Every country has its preferences for greens, and they are plentiful on dining tables. For example, Greeks use lettuce leaves as a "green wrap" to encase. vegetables, meat, and grains. A popular appetizer is horta, which is a mix of herbs served with oil or lightly sautéed. The fondness for spinach comes from France, whose mild flavor makes it suitable for both main dishes and culinary fillings. Italians enjoy broccoli, especially its most nutritious part — the leaves. They consume it raw,

balancing its robust flavor with tomatoes and cheese, or sauté it with balsamic vinegar for added taste.

Dairy Products...

Dairy products remain highly popular in Mediterranean countries. Animal milk provides calcium, vitamin D, protein, and amino acids. While France favors aged and mature cheeses, Greece is a true fan of yogurt, serving it with salads, meats, baked goods, and as a standalone dish, often paired with fruits or herbs.

Among the most nutritious cheeses are:

• Dietary goat cheese, is low in calories but high in B vitamins, trace minerals, and easily digestible proteins.
• Feta cheese, made from sheep's or goat's milk, is known for regulating blood pressure, soothing the nervous system, and strengthening bones.
• Sharp parmesan, is rich in protein, vitamins, and amino acids.
• Silky provolone, is enhanced with beneficial enzymes that give it distinctive flavors.

Greek yogurt is a nutrient-rich dairy product that offers several health benefits. Here is a more detailed overview of the nutrition value of Greek yogurt:

- High protein content, which is essential for muscle growth, repair, and overall body maintenance.
- Probiotics, which are beneficial bacteria that support gut health and digestion. Probiotics help maintain a healthy balance of microflora in the gut, which can contribute to better overall digestive health.
- Good source of calcium, a mineral that is crucial for maintaining strong bones and teeth.
- Provides various essential vitamins and minerals, such as vitamin B12, potassium, and phosphorus.

Vegetables..

It's no surprise that Mediterranean countries offer diverse salads on their menus. Nutritionists have long stressed the importance of incorporating a variety of vegetables into the daily diet, as this can enhance digestion and heart health.

When minimally processed, fresh vegetables olive oil, and aromatic herbs' flavor, provide a rich source of vitamins, organic acids, carbohydrates, proteins, and fats — everything essential for the body.

Adding a few slices of feta cheese, creates an authentic Greek salad, a signature dish of Mediterranean cuisine.

A vital aspect of the Mediterranean diet is the decrease in saturated animal fats, replaced.

Fats...

Mediterrianian diet is well-known by healthier plant oils and unsaturated fats. Examples of plant oils include olive oil, nuts, and seeds. Fatty fish are rich in unsaturated fats and are an excellent source of polyunsaturated omega-3 fatty acids. These fatty acids help maintain the balance of vitamins and trace minerals in the body and contribute to healthy, supple skin and shiny hair.

Olive oil...

Olive oil is especially significant in the Mediterranean diet. Incorporating several tablespoons of olive oil daily is a fundamental aspect of this unique approach to healthy eating. There's no need for concern — some nutritionists suggest including 60 grams of bread soaked in 40 grams of olive oil for breakfast each day. This is quite reasonable, as the fats in olive oil are similar to those in breast milk, making it a recommended choice for introducing plant oils during complementary feeding.

For adult food enthusiasts, olive oil enhances bone mineralization, supports digestion, and helps stabilize blood pressure. It contains oleic acid (up to 70% of its composition), classified as an Omega-9 unsaturated fatty acid and a potent natural antioxidant. This leads to improved metabolism and a slowing of the aging process. Additionally, olive oil is abundant in vitamins E and K, which aid in regulating immune function and energy processes in the body.

However, it's crucial to recognize that not all olive oil is produced to proper standards. Many dishonest producers saturate the market with low-quality and counterfeit oils. These products may be extracted and processed through improper methods that compromise delicate nutrients, and some fatty acids can even turn rancid or become toxic.

Therefore, selecting only high-quality oil labeled as "extra virgin" and, ideally, cold-pressed is wise. The distinctiveness of olive oil lies in its capacity to be consumed raw without any processing.

For those fortunate enough to cultivate olives in their area, they can manually harvest the ripe fruits, carefully hand-press them to extract the precious oil, and savor the rich.

Meat and Fish...

Examining the balance between meat and fish dishes reveals that, despite delicacies such as Parma ham from Italy and jamón from Spain, fish and seafood are predominant. Red meat is infrequently found on menus, as seafood offers the most significant quantities of saturated fatty acids, vitamins, and trace minerals.

Spices, Seasonings, and Aromatic Oils..................

Mediterranean cuisine is significantly enriched by aromatic oils infused with herbs and spices. You can easily prepare these at home — garlic-infused oil pairs perfectly with pasta and sauces, mint oil elevates the freshness of salads, and lemon oil adds a touch of elegance to fish dishes.

Additionally, this approach significantly lowers salt intake, which contributes to the beneficial effects on the cardiovascular system in particular, as well as the overall health of the body.

Don't hesitate to incorporate spices and seasonings into your recipes, and feel free to experiment with different combinations and amounts.

Red Wine...

Another enjoyable feature of the Mediterranean diet is the inclusion of red wine, a staple that encapsulates the concept of moderation in alcohol consumption, aligning with the diet's overall emphasis on balance and enjoyment. Consuming a daily amount of 10 to 50 ml of red wine can not only add a delightful touch to meals but also offer potential benefits such as enhancing heart health, promoting the cleansing of blood vessels, and uplifting one's spirits, reflecting the holistic approach to well-being inherent in the Mediterranean lifestyle. Enjoy!

The benefits of the Mediterranean diet.

The foods in this diet are minimally processed and contain no added refined sugars. They include olive oil, a variety of vegetables and fruits, legumes, nuts, whole grain products, and small portions of animal products that are always "organic" and have a short shelf life. There are almost no GMOs, artificial ingredients, preservatives, flavor enhancers, or sugar.

For desserts, people in the Mediterranean often enjoy fruits or light homemade sweets made with natural sweeteners like honey. The animal component of the diet features moderate amounts of cow, goat, or sheep cheese and yogurt, along with a significant intake of locally caught fish.

This offers a source of omega-3 fatty acids and other beneficial fats, which help to increase "good" cholesterol and strengthen the walls of blood vessels.

Cardiovascular Health Improvement....................

 A high intake of monounsaturated fats and foods rich in omega-3s is associated with significantly reducing mortality from all causes, especially heart disease. Numerous studies have demonstrated the positive effects of the Mediterranean diet, which is rich in alpha-linolenic acid (ALA) from olive oil, particularly a 30 percent decrease in the risk of cardiovascular-related death and a 45 percent reduction in acute heart failure.

Additionally, research from Warwick Medical School has shown that individuals who regularly consume extra virgin olive oil experience more significant reductions in blood pressure compared to those who predominantly use sunflower oil.

Moreover, among Mediterranean residents, the problem of low levels of "good" cholesterol is infrequent, as they typically obtain a high amount of healthy fats from their natural diet.

Healthy Weight Loss...

This diet enables you to enjoy various delicious foods without feeling hungry. As a result, you can adhere to this eating pattern for an extended period without any setbacks, allowing you to manage your weight and reduce fat intake gently and naturally.

The Mediterranean diet is flexible, whether you prefer to increase your carbohydrate consumption or emphasize high-quality protein sources from both animal and, particularly, plant origins. This eating style will help you regulate weight gain, maintain stable blood sugar levels, enhance your mood, and sustain high energy levels.

Cancer Prevention..

Research conducted by the Department of Surgery at the University of Genoa, Italy, indicates that a balanced ratio of essential fatty acids omega-6 and omega-3, along with a high intake of fiber, antioxidants, and polyphenols found in fruits, vegetables, olive oil, and wine, safeguards DNA from damage, prevents cell mutations, reduces inflammation, and inhibits tumor growth. Moreover, olive oil is associated with decreased colon and intestinal cancer risk.

Treatment and Prevention of Diabetes.................

The Mediterranean diet helps regulate excess insulin, the hormone responsible for managing blood sugar levels, contributing to weight gain and maintaining weight even when following a diet. A wealth of evidence indicates that the Mediterranean diet can serve as an anti-inflammatory dietary approach, potentially assisting in the management of conditions linked to chronic inflammation, including metabolic syndrome. A low-sugar diet emphasizing fresh foods and healthy fats is essential for a natural lifestyle among diabetics. The Mediterranean die helps maintain stable blood sugar levels by preventing spikes and dips. Carbohydrates from whole grain bread.

Cognitive Health Protection and Boosting Mood

It is well-established that healthy fats, such as olive oil and nuts, play a significant role in combating age-related declines in cognitive abilities. These fats can help mitigate the detrimental effects of toxins, free radicals, poor nutrition that leads to inflammation, and food allergies, all of which can impair brain function. Cognitive disorders may develop when the brain lacks sufficient dopamine, an essential chemical for proper bodily movement, mood regulation, and mental processes.

Probiotic-rich foods, such as yogurt and kefir, contribute to healthy digestive function, which is also associated with cognitive health. As a result, the Mediterranean dietary approach may act as a natural means of treating and preventing such diseases as Parkinson's disease, Alzheimer's disease, and age-related dementia.

It supports longevity..

In 1988, a study was conducted in Lyon where patients who had suffered heart attacks were instructed to follow either a Mediterranean diet rich in monounsaturated fats or a standard diet significantly reducing saturated fats. Four years after the study began, follow-up results revealed that participants in the Mediterranean diet group had 70% fewer heart-related issues and a 45% lower risk of death from any cause compared to those on the standard diet. Additionally, there was minimal difference in total cholesterol levels, indicating no direct link between cholesterol and heart disease. The results were so remarkable that the study was ethically halted early, allowing all participants to continue with the Mediterranean diet for optimal health and longevity.

Helps Relieve Stress and Promote Relaxation......

Chronic stress takes a heavy toll on quality of life, significantly impacts weight management, and has negative implications for overall health. Embracing the Mediterranean diet encourages increased exposure to nature, promotes adequate rest, and thus provides a holistic solution for stress relief, ultimately leading to the reduction of inflammatory responses. Additionally, it creates opportunities for more laughter, dance, relaxation, and the pursuit of personal interests, contributing to a more balanced and fulfilling lifestyle.

Combating Depression...

A 2018 study published in the journal Molecular Psychiatry revealed that adhering to a Mediterranean diet can lower the risk of depression. Inflammation is commonly recognized as a critical factor in many disorders and mental health issues, including schizophrenia, obsessive-compulsive disorder, depression, anxiety, fatigue, and social withdrawal. Conversely, a nutrient-rich diet safeguards the brain from organic and functional changes, highlighting the importance of a holistic approach to mental well-being. Additionally, modifications in dietary habits and lifestyle — such as ensuring sufficient sleep, engaging in mindful eating, planning meals ahead, and managing stress — play significant roles in sustaining mental health stability and promoting overall wellness.

Notes ....
....
....
....
....
....
....
....
....
....

What should you eat, and how often?

If you've decided to embrace this popular and essentially unique dietary system, your daily meals should now feature the following foods:

Fresh fruits (such as apples, bananas, pears, citrus fruits, figs, peaches, apricots, berries, melons, and watermelons);

Whole grains (including brown rice, rye, barley, corn, buckwheat, whole oats, wheat, and products made from these grains — like bread and pasta);

Legumes and beans (such as lentils, chickpeas, beans, peas, and peanuts);

Root vegetables (including sweet potatoes, turnips, yams, parsnips, and Jerusalem artichokes);

Nuts and seeds (like walnuts, almonds, hazelnuts, macadamia nuts, cashews, sesame seeds, sunflower seeds, and pumpkin seeds);

Spices and herbs (such as garlic, nutmeg, cinnamon, pepper, basil, mint, rosemary, and sage)— these will significantly help reduce the amount of salt in your diet;

Plant-based fats (like olive oil pure avocado, and well as oil derived from avocado);

Aim for approximately **2 liters of clean water** daily. Tea or coffee is acceptable, but avoid sweetened drinks and fruit juices;

Dairy products, including cheese, yogurt, or kefir, should be enjoyed in moderation;

Red wine may be included in moderation (although it is optional).

Each week, the following are necessary:

Red wine may be included in moderation (although it is optional).

Fish and seafood, with a preference for wild-caught varieties over farmed ones; shrimp, oysters, mollusks, mussels, and crabs should be included at least 4 times a week;

Eggs should be consumed in moderation, 2-4 times a week;

Potatoes should be eaten moderately;

A small amount of **sweets**.

You can consume the following every month:

Red meat;

Poultry (such as chicken, duck, and turkey) and lean meats (including rabbit, ham, and pork tenderloin).

It's advisable to steer clear of the following in your diet:

Refined sugars and products that contain them (such as ice cream, candies, soft drinks, and table sugar);

Highly processed grains (including white bread, pasta made from soft wheat, and polished grains);

Trans fats (found in margarine and related products);

Refined oils (all varieties, including soybean, canola, and cottonseed oils);

Processed meat products (like sausages, deli meats, and convenience items);

Foods that have been further processed or enriched (marked as "fat-free," "enriched," or "refined").

Product Index

110	Beer
100	Glucose, modified starch, toasted white bread
95	Sweet rolls, fried potatoes
90	White rice
85	Popcorn, boiled carrots
85	Pumpkin, zucchini, watermelon
83	Mashed potatoes
71	Millet
70	Milk chocolate, sugar
69	Wheat flour
66	Pineapple
65	Orange juice, maple syrup, marmalade, raisins, whole grain bread
64	Macaroni and cheese
60	Banana, melon, ice cream, mayonnaise, oatmeal, cocoa with sugar

59	Canned corn
55	Grape juice, ketchup
50	Kiwi, mango, apple juice, brown rice
45	Canned green peas, coconut
40	Prunes, dried apricots, carrot juice
35	Apple, chickpeas, orange, fat-free yogurt
34	Beans
30	Apricot, grapefruit, carrot, tomato, blackberries, blueberries, dark chocolate
25	Cherry, raspberry, strawberry
15	Almonds, broccoli, cucumber, spinach, mushrooms, walnuts, soy
10	Avocado
9	Leafy lettuce
5	Herbs and spices
0	Meat, poultry, fish, eggs

Disadvantages and Harm of the Diet

One of the main disadvantages of this dietary system is the need to alter one's eating habits — specifically, to eliminate many processed and refined foods in favor of higher-quality, often more expensive products available in our region. It is still unclear whether the more significant obstacle will be the cost or the adjustment from the previous diet. Furthermore, this diet may not suit individuals with specific seafood allergies or intolerances.

People with stomach or intestinal ulcers should also approach the meal selection cautiously, considering the high fiber content of the daily menu.

Additionally, pregnant women and others who may be negatively affected by even small amounts of alcohol should refrain from consuming the red wine that the diet permits. Many people question whether it's possible to lose weight on this diet. This gentle approach doesn't yield immediate results.

It may not be appropriate for those looking to address severe obesity. If the main aim of the diet is weight loss, it's crucial to include physical activity as part of the plan. Furthermore, not all diets with restrictions allow for practical training and exercise.

One appealing aspect of the Mediterranean diet is that it provides the energy needed for physical activity, which improves weight loss results, helps shape a toned and attractive physique, and enhances overall health.

The lack of a strict menu may seem inconvenient for those opting to lose weight with this method. You must track your calorie intake to ensure you don't feel hungry while still shedding pounds. You must manage the relationship between your physical activity and food consumption independently. Many diet supporters appreciate this flexibility, as strict limitations can be more challenging to maintain.

Notes

Breakfast

Hot Mediterranean sandwich

♦ 4 servings
♦ 15 min
♦ 7 ingredients

Nutritional value per serving:

Calories: **538 kcal**
Proteins: **16 grams**
Fats: **44 grams**
Carbohydrates: **23 grams**

Ingredients:

• Cherry tomatoes*: 500 g
• Mozzarella cheese: 200 g
• Toast bread: 4 slices
• Pesto: 12 tablespoons

• Arugula: to taste
• Salt: to taste
• Ground black pepper: to taste

Cooking instructions:

1. Preheat the oven to 200°C (392°F)

2. Remove the mozzarella from its packaging and allow the excess liquid to drain. Slice it into thin pieces.

3. Cut the cherry tomatoes in half.

4. Spread the pesto sauce on the toast and place the slices on a baking sheet lined with parchment paper. Then, layer the tomatoes and cheese on top of the toast. Add a little more pesto sauce on top.

5. Bake the sandwiches in the oven for 8-10 min or until the cheese melts.

6. Once the sandwiches are ready, sprinkle a little salt and pepper and garnish with chopped arugula.

*Cherry tomatoes can easily be substituted with regular tomatoes without compromising the flavor. You can use either home-made or store-bought pesto sauce.

Sandwiches with lightly salted salmon and avocado

- ◆ 1 servings
- ◆ 10 min
- ◆ 5 ingredients

Nutritional value per serving:
Calories: **502 kcal**
Proteins: **5 grams**
Fats: **18 grams**
Carbohydrates: **48 grams**

Ingredients:

- Avocado: 1 piece
- Bread or croissant: 1 piece
- Lime juice: to taste
- Green onion: to taste
- Olive oil: to taste

Cooking instructions:

1. Toast the bread or croissant and warm it in the oven for 2 minutes.

2. Drizzle with olive oil.

3. Peel the avocado, slice it, and finely chop the green onion.

4. Place the avocado and green onions in a blender. Add lime juice and olive oil, then blend until smooth.

5. Slice the salmon into thin pieces and remove any bones.

6. Spread the avocado mixture on each piece of toast.

7. Top each slice with salmon and garnish with green onions if desired.

Notes

Bruschetta with sun-dried to-matoes, mozzarella, and olives

- ◆ 4 servings
- ◆ 15 min
- ◆ 5 ingredients

Nutritional value per serving:

Calories: **209 kcal**

Proteins: **8,5 grams**

Fats: **5 grams**

Carbohydrates: **32 grams**

Ingredients:

- Mozzarella: 200 g
- Sun-dried tomatoes: 100 g
- Pitted olives: 50 g
- Basil: to taste
- Ciabatta or bread: 8 pieces

Cooking instructions:

1. Preheat the oven to 200 °C (392 °F). Line a baking sheet with parchment paper.

2. Chop the sun-dried tomatoes and olives.

3. Place the tomatoes and olives on top. Bake for 5-10 minutes or until the mozzarella melts. Garnish with basil.

4. On the prepared bruschetta, place the mozzarella on top after breaking it in half.

5. You can drizzle with soy sauce.

Notes

Bruschetta with egg

◆ 1 servings
◆ 7 min
◆ 8 ingredients

Nutritional value per serving:
Calories: **298 kcal**
Proteins: **12 grams**
Fats: **20 grams**
Carbohydrates: **20 grams**

Ingredients:

• Ciabatta: 1 piece
• Tomato: 1 piece
• Avocado flesh: 30 g
• Cream cheese: 30 g

• Dijon mustard: 20 g
• Lemon: 1 clove
• Egg: 1 piece
• Black pepper, chili flakes, and sea salt: to taste

Cooking instructions:

1. Place a slice of ciabatta on a dry, hot skillet.

2. Once the bread is lightly toasted, flip it over. Remove from the heat after one minute.

3. Mash the avocado with a fork and add lemon juice. Add salt.

4. Spread cream cheese on the bruschetta and sprinkle with black pepper. Add mustard on top.

5. Spread avocado on the bruschetta.

6. Top with a poached egg. Season with salt and sprinkle with chili flakes.

Notes

Sandwich with caramelized turkey

- ◆ 4 servings
- ◆ 20 min
- ◆ 10 ingredients

Nutritional value per serving:

Calories: **365 kcal**
Proteins: **19 grams**
Fats: **25 grams**
Carbohydrates: **24 grams**

Ingredients:

- Mushrooms: 3 pieces
- Bread: 4 pieces
- Cheese: 150 g
- Brown sugar: 20 g
- Smoked paprika: 5 g
- Ground dried garlic: 5 g
- Soy sauce: 20 ml
- Balsamic vinegar: 10 ml
- Turkey thigh fillet: 300 g
- Meat spices and salt: to taste

Cooking instructions:

1. Slice the meat and coat it in spices (smoked paprika, ground dried garlic, meat spices, sugar). Place the pieces in a skillet over medium heat, being sure to watch that the sugar doesn't burn.

2. Spread grated cheese on the bread and toast it in the oven at 180 degrees Celsius for 2 minutes.

3. Slice the mushrooms and transfer them to a deep bowl. Add balsamic vinegar, soy sauce, and dry broth seasoning, and let it marinate for about 15 minutes. Then, sauté the mushrooms until the liquid reduces to a sauce.

4. Place the meat on the bread with cheese, add the mushrooms, and drizzle with sauce.

Notes

Eggplant sandwich with avocado

- ◆ 2 servings
- ◆ 15 min
- ◆ 8 ingredients

Nutritional value per serving:
Calories: **300 kcal**
Proteins: **10 grams**
Fats: **16 grams**
Carbohydrates: **28 grams**

Ingredients:

- Eggplants: 1 piece
- Avocado: 1 piece
- Cream cheese: 70 g
- Garlic: 3 cloves
- Tomato: 5 g
- Lime: ¼ piece
- Olive oil and flour for breading the eggplants
- Salt: to taste

Cooking instructions:

1. Slice the eggplant into 1 cm thick rounds and soak them in lightly salted water.

2. Mash the avocado flesh in a deep bowl with a fork. Peel the garlic and press it into a bowl with the avocado using a garlic press. Add cream cheese to the bowl and squeeze lime juice on top.

3. Add salt and mix well.

4. Olive oil and flour for breading the eggplants. Fry for 4-5 minutes on each side.

5. Pat the eggplants dry with a paper towel.

6. Slice the tomato into rounds about 6–8 mm thick.

7. Spread the avocado filling on the eggplant.

8. Place the tomato slices on top. Spread the avocado filling on the eggplant again. Garnish with diced tomato on top and your favorite herbs.

Notes

Ciabatta with roasted vegetables, arugula, and chicken

◆ 1 servings
◆ 25 min
◆ 10 ingredients

Nutritional value per serving:

Calories: **260 kcal**
Proteins: **15 grams**
Fats: **18 grams**
Carbohydrates: **35 grams**

Ingredients:

- Ciabatta: 1 piece
- Sweet pepper: 1 piece
- Sweet pepper: 1 piece
- Cherry tomatoes: 5 pieces
- Pitted olives: to taste

- Chicken fillet: 200 g
- Arugula: 20 g
- Fresh thyme: 1 sprig
- Olive oil: 20 g
- Sea salt to taste: to taste

Cooking instructions:

1. Drizzle olive oil into a baking dish. Add the sliced vegetables a few garlic cloves (you can leave them unpeeled), and sprigs of thyme. Season with salt. Roast in a preheated oven for about 20 min at 180°C.

2. Grill the chicken pieces in a grill pan.

3. Slice the ciabatta lengthwise into two halves, brush with olive oil, and toast in the oven or on a pan. On one half, layer the roasted vegetables, a few slices, and arugula, then drizzle with the juice from the vegetables. Cover with the second half of the ciabatta.

Notes

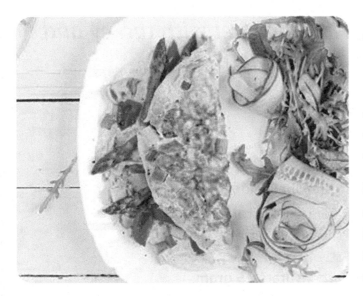

Mediterranean omelet

◆ 2 servings
◆ 10 min
◆ 13 ingredients

Nutritional value per serving:

Calories: **205 kcal**
Proteins: **14 grams**
Fats: **14 grams**
Carbohydrates: **6 grams**

Ingredients:

• Parmesan cheese: 10 g
• Mushrooms: 20 g
• Onion: 10 g
• Sweet pepper: 10 g
• Sun-dried tomatoes: 15 g
• Feta cheese: 30 g
• Olives: 20 g

• Oranges: 20 g
• Parsley: 5 g
• Olive oil: 20 g
• Sea salt to taste: to taste
• Milk: 50 ml
• Egg: 2 pieces

Cooking instructions:

1. Dice the mushrooms, pepper, and onion. Place them in a heated skillet with vegetable oil and sauté until golden brown. Then, add the sun-dried tomatoes, olives, orange pulp, and parsley.

2. Whisk the milk with the eggs and pour it evenly over the sautéed vegetables. Cook the omelet on both sides until done.

3. Place the feta in the center of the omelet, then roll it up. Sprinkle grated Parmesan on top.

Notes

Fluffy omelet with turkey and green onions

◆ 2 servings
◆ 30 min
◆ 8 ingredients

Nutritional value per serving:
Calories: **196 kcal**
Proteins: **14 grams**
Fats: **13 grams**
Carbohydrates: **5 grams**

Ingredients:

- Chicken eggs: 3 pieces
- Turkey: 150 g
- Green Onion: 10 g
- Tomatoes: 1 piece

- Ground pepper mix: to taste
- Olive oil: 20 g
- Sea salt to taste: to taste
- Milk: 170 ml

Cooking instructions:

1. Grease the dish with olive oil, place tomato slices on the bottom, then add grilled turkey and green onions.

2. Mix the eggs with milk, add salt and pepper, and don't over— whisk.

3. Pour the egg mixture over the filling in the dish and place it in the oven. Bake at 400°F.

Notes

Morning pie with oats, bananas, and blueberries

◆ 4 servings
◆ 60 min
◆ 10 ingredients

Nutritional value per serving:
Calories: **331 kcal**
Proteins: **9 grams**
Fats: **9 grams**
Carbohydrates: **56 grams**

Ingredients:

- Bananas: 2 pieces
- Blueberries: 1 cup
- Honey: 3 tablespoons
- Walnuts: 20 g
- Oats: 1 cup
- Milk: 200ml
- Cinnamon: ⅓ teaspoon
- Chicken egg: 1 piece
- Vanilla: 1 teaspoon
- Powdered sugar 1 teaspoon

Cooking instructions:

1. Preheat the oven to 190°C. Take a baking dish and line the bottom and sides with foil.

2. Slice the bananas into rounds and place them in the prepared dish. Add half of the blueberries, 1/4 teaspoon of cinnamon, and 1 tablespoon of honey. Cover with foil and bake for 15 minutes until the bananas soften.

3. Next, mix the oats, half of the walnuts, baking powder, and the remaining cinnamon in a bowl. In a separate bowl, whisk together the remaining honey, milk, eggs, and vanilla.

4. Return the dish to the oven and bake for 30-35 minutes, until the top is golden and the mixture is set. Let it cool slightly before serving.

5. Bake the pie for about 30 minutes, or until a golden-brown crust form on top. For garnish, sprinkle with powdered sugar. Serve warm.

Notes

Greek bowl

◆ 2 servings

◆ 15 min

◆ 12 ingredients

Nutritional value per serving:

Calories: **380 kcal**

Proteins: **4,28 grams**

Fats: **9 grams**

Carbohydrates: **4 grams**

Ingredients:

- Eggs: 2 pieces
- Feta cheese: 60 g
- Arugula: 120 g
- Cucumber: 1 piece
- Tomato: 1 piece
- Red sweet pepper: 200 ml

- Cinnamon: 1/3 teaspoon
- Olives: 8 pieces
- Olive oil: 2 tablespoons
- Dried parsley: 2 teaspoons
- Salt: to taste
- Freshly ground black pepper to taste

Cooking instructions:

1. Boil the eggs for 7 minutes and let them cool.

2. Slice the tomato, cucumber, and sweet pepper. Crumble the feta cheese. In a large bowl, combine the vegetables and arugula, drizzle with olive oil, season with salt, dried parsley, and freshly ground black pepper. Gently toss to combine.

3. Peel the eggs and cut each in half. Divide the salad into bowls, adding egg halves and olives to each, and serve immediately.

Notes

Toast with ricotta and straw-berries .

- ◆ 2 servings
- ◆ 15 min
- ◆ 7 ingredients

Nutritional value per serving:

Calories: **355 kcal**
Proteins: **5 grams**
Fats: **4 grams**
Carbohydrates: **21 grams**

Ingredients:

- Bread slices: 4 pieces
- Strawberries: 800 g
- Ricotta: 200 g
- Honey: 3 tablespoons

- Basil: 2 sprigs
- Vanilla sugar: 1 teaspoon
- Salt: to taste

Cooking instructions:

1. Preheat the oven to 190 °C. Remove the hulls from the strawberries. Cut large berries into 2–4 pieces, leaving the small ones whole. Toast the bread slices in a toaster. Separate the basil leaves from the stems.

2. Place the berries in a large oven-safe dish, drizzle with 2 tablespoons of liquid honey, add a pinch of salt and vanilla sugar, and gently mix. Put the dish with the berries on the middle rack of the oven and bake for 10 minutes.

3. Spread ricotta on the toast and top with the roasted berries. Garnish with basil and drizzle with the syrup from the dish and the remaining honey.

Notes

Frittata with vegetables

◆ 2 servings
◆ 20 min
◆ 8 ingredients

Nutritional value per serving:
Calories: **355 kcal**
Proteins: **5 grams**
Fats: **12 grams**
Carbohydrates: **8 grams**

Ingredients:

• Eggs: 4 pieces
• Sweet potato: 1 big piece
• Cherry tomatoes: 200 g
• Spinach: 200 g

• Mushrooms: 4-5 pieces
• Olive oil: 5 tablespoons
• Salt: to taste
• Freshly ground black pepper: to taste

Cooking instructions:

1. To prepare the vegetable frittata, slice the sweet potato and mushrooms into thin rounds. Halve the cherry tomatoes. In a large, non-stick skillet, heat the vegetable oil and add the potatoes, seasoning them lightly with salt. Cook over medium heat, covered, for 7 minutes.

2. Meanwhile, in a bowl, beat the eggs and season with salt and freshly ground black pepper. Pour the egg mixture over the vegetables, ensuring even distribution once the vegetables are cooked. Reduce the heat to low and cook until the edges start to set about 5 minutes. You can finish cooking it under a broiler for a couple of minutes to set the top if desired.

3. Remove the tough stems from the spinach, add the leaves to the vegetables, and heat for 1 min. In a bowl, crack the eggs, season with salt and pepper, and whisk. Pour the eggs into the skillet and stir. Cook until the eggs are set, about 5 minutes. Cut the frittata into portions and serve hot.

Notes

Tortilla with potatoes and cara-melized onions

- ◆ 4 servings
- ◆ 20 min
- ◆ 13 ingredients

Nutritional value per serving:

Calories: **235 kcal**
Proteins: **7 grams**
Fats: **19 grams**
Carbohydrates: **7 grams**

Ingredients:

- Eggs: 6 pieces
- Potatos: 500 g
- Grated Parmesan cheese: 60 g
- Cream: 2 tablespoons
- Thyme: 2 sprigs
- Olive oil: 4 tablespoons
- Salt: to taste

- Freshly ground black pepper: to taste
- Large red onion: 1 piece
- White dry wine: 50 ml
- Wine vinegar: 2 tablespoons
- Olive oil: 3 tablespoons
- Honey: 2 teaspoons

Cooking instructions:

1. Slice the onion into rings. In a skillet, heat the olive oil and add the onion. Cook over low heat, stirring, for 10 minutes. Season with salt, add the wine, wine vinegar, and honey, and cook for another 7 min.

2. Peel the potatoes and slice them into thin rounds, then soak them in hot water, add salt, and boil for 5 minutes. Drain the water and dry the potatoes.

3. Combine the eggs with half of the grated Parmesan cheese and the cream in a large bowl. Add the thyme leaves, salt, and pepper, and mix thoroughly.

4. In a skillet, heat the olive oil. Fry the potatoes on all sides until golden brown, about 5 minutes, then reduce the heat to low. Pour the egg mixture into the skillet, cover with a lid, and cook for 10 min.

5. Once the eggs are set, the tortilla is ready. Remove from heat, sprinkle with the remaining Parmesan cheese, and top with the caramelized onions.

Notes

Quinoa porridge

- ◆ 4 servings
- ◆ 20 min
- ◆ 11 ingredients

Nutritional value per serving:
Calories: **235 kcal**
Proteins: **7 grams**
Fats: **19 grams**
Carbohydrates: **7 grams**

Ingredients:

- Almond milk (you can use rice or coconut milk): 1 cup
- Quinoa flakes: ⅓ cup
- Blueberries: ¼ cup
- Cream: 2 tablespoons
- Thyme: 2 sprigs
- Olive oil: 4 tablespoons
- Salt: to taste
- Peanut butter, honey: 1 tablespoon
- Fresh strawberries: 50 g
- Fresh blackberries: 50 g
- Chia seeds: 1 tablespoons

Cooking instructions:

1. Pour almond milk into a medium-sized saucepan and heat over medium heat.

2. When the milk starts to boil, add 1/3 cup of quinoa flakes, 1/4 cup of goji berries (or dried blueberries), and a pinch of salt. If you are cooking whole quinoa, boil it longer according to the package instructions.

3. Turn off the heat and stir the flakes.

4. Let the flakes sit for 3 minutes to allow the quinoa to thoroughly cook.

5. Stir the grains again. Its consistency should be thicker and creamier.

6. Serve the flakes on a plate and top with your favorite ingredients.

7. If you want to make it even healthier, add 2 tablespoons of chia seeds.

Notes

Toast with cheese, honey, and pear

◆ 2 servings
◆ 10 min
◆ 5 ingredients

Nutritional value per serving:

Calories: **260 kcal**
Proteins: **7 grams**
Fats: **8 grams**
Carbohydrates: **15 grams**

Ingredients:

• Toasted whole grain bread: 4 pieces
• Cream cheese (e.g., Philadelphia): 100 g
• Pears: 2 piece
• Honey: 4 teaspoons
• Grated almonds: ¼ cup

Cooking instructions:

1. Spread a piece of cheese on each slice of bread.

2. Add pear slices on top of the cheese.

3. Drizzle with honey and garnish with grated almonds.

Notes

Healthy waffles

- ◆ 1 servings
- ◆ 10 min
- ◆ 6 ingredients

Nutritional value per serving:

Calories: **330 kcal**

Proteins: **12 grams**

Fats: **10 grams**

Carbohydrates: **26 grams**

Ingredients:

- Egg: 1 piece
- Egg whites: 30 g
- Shredded mozzarella: 100 g
- Ground almonds or almond flour: 1 tablespoon
- Salt: ½ teaspoon
- Black pepper and spices or herbs: to taste

Cooking instructions:

1. In a bowl, mix the egg and egg whites.

2. Add the shredded mozzarella, ground almonds or almond flour, salt, black pepper, and spices.

3. Stir well until the mixture is smooth.

4. Preheat the waffle maker and pour the batter into it.

5. Cook the waffles for 3-5 minutes until golden and crispy.

6. Serve hot with your favorite keto toppings.

Notes

Oatmeal with pear, blue cheese, and cinnamon

◆ 2 servings
◆ 10 min
◆ 6 ingredients

Nutritional value per serving:

Calories: **330 kcal**
Proteins: **12 grams**
Fats: **10 grams**
Carbohydrates: **26 grams**

Ingredients:

• Oats: 1 cup
• Pears: 2 pieces
• Blue cheese (such as Dorblu): 50 g

• Cinnamon: ½ teaspoon
• Honey: 2 tablespoons
• Milk (or water): 2 tablespoons

Cooking instructions:

1. Heat the milk or water in a small saucepan and bring it to a boil.

2. Add the oats and cook over medium heat, stirring occasionally, for about 5-7 minutes until the oatmeal is soft.

3. Peel and slice the pears into thin slices.

4. Stir the pear slices, honey, and cinnamon into the cooked oatmeal.

5. Top with pieces of blue cheese and garnish with remaining pear slices.

6. Serve warm, enjoying the balance of sweetness and tangy flavors.

Notes

Granola

- ◆ 4 servings
- ◆ 45 min
- ◆ 5 ingredients

Nutritional value per serving:
Calories: **443 kcal**
Proteins: **8 grams**
Fats: **12 grams**
Carbohydrates: **35 grams**

Ingredients:

- Rolled oats: 300 g
- Nuts: 150 g
- Dried fruits: 100 g
- Honey: 2.5 tablespoons
- Olive oil: 2.5 tablespoons

Cooking instructions:

1. Chop the nuts (I used walnuts) with a knife or crush them with a mallet.

2. Rinse the dried fruits (raisins, cranberries, or apricots) well and soak them in warm water. I chose light seedless raisins.

3. In a deep bowl, mix the oatmeal and chopped nuts.

4. Mix by hand, thoroughly combining the dry ingredients with the honey and oil. You should end up with a reasonably sticky mixture that looks like clumps.

5. Spread the granola onto a baking dish or tray. It's okay to line the dish with parchment paper.

6. Preheat the oven to 265-300 degrees Fahrenheit). Bake the oats for 30-35 minutes.

7. Stir the granola with a spoon or wooden spatula every 7-8 minutes. This is very important! The granola should bake evenly and thoroughly.

8. Five minutes before the granola is done, add the dried raisins or cranberries that have been dried on paper towels. After taking it out of the oven, it may seem like the granola is moist, but it will become crunchy and crumbly as it cools down.

9. Enjoy the granola with yogurt or milk (hot or cold), fresh berries and fruits.

Quinoa with vegetables

♦ 2 servings
♦ 45 min
♦ 10 ingredients

Nutritional value per serving:
Calories: **390 kcal**
Proteins: **15 grams**
Fats: **10 grams**
Carbohydrates: **18 grams**

Ingredients:

• Water: 2 cup
• Quinoa: 1 cup
• Zucchini: 1 piece
• Carrot: 1 piece
• Celery: 1 piece

• Garlic: 2 cloves
• Olive oil: 2 tablespoons
• Dried basil: to taste
• Salt: to taste
• Black pepper: to taste

Cooking instructions:

1. Rinse the quinoa thoroughly, then add it to water in a 1:2 ratio and bring to a boil.

2. Add salt to taste, cover with a lid, and simmer on low heat until cooked.

3. Let it sit for 5-10 minutes.

4. Wash and dice the vegetables.

5. In a heated skillet, pour in 3-4 tablespoons of olive oil and sauté the vegetables, stirring occasionally, for 15-20 minutes.

6. Season with dried basil, salt, and pepper towards the end of cooking.

7. Mix and add the vegetables to the quinoa.

Notes

Croissants with omelette à la Agnès Sorel

◆ 2 servings
◆ 45 min
◆ 10 ingredients

Nutritional value per serving:

Calories: **310 kcal**
Proteins: **31 grams**
Fats: **43 grams**
Carbohydrates: **48 grams**

Ingredients:

- Eggs: 2 pieces
- Croissant: 4 pieces
- Butter: 20 g
- White wine vinegar: 20 ml
- Mushrooms: 100 g

- Chicken fillet: 200 g
- Olive oil: 2 tablespoons
- Sugar: 20g
- Salt: to taste
- Black pepper: to taste

Cooking instructions:

1. Sauté the diced mushrooms, chicken fillet, and veal tongue in butter. Drizzle the skillet with vinegar, season with salt and pepper, and simmer for a couple of minutes.

2. After that, pour the dish with lightly beaten eggs, season with salt and pepper, add sugar, and cook over low heat with the lid on until set.

3. Warm the croissants in the microwave, oven, or on a dry skillet, cut off the tops, and fill them with the omelet.

Notes

Broccoli and cheese pancakes

♦ 4 servings
♦ 20 min
♦ 8 ingredients

Nutritional value per serving:

Calories: **130 kcal**
Proteins: **8 grams**
Fats: **14 grams**
Carbohydrates: **17 grams**

Ingredients:

• Broccoli: 250 g
• Wheat flour: 70 g
• Egg: 1 piece
• Grated Parmesan cheese: 30 g

• Salt: to taste
• Black pepper: to taste
• Garlic: 1 clove
• Yogurt: 100 g

Cooking instructions:

1. Boil the broccoli in salted water, then drain it in a colander and blend it until smooth.

2. In a separate bowl, beat the egg, then add flour, salt, pepper, and cheese. Mix with the broccoli. Heat oil in a skillet, shape into pancakes, and fry for 3 minutes on each side. Serve with yogurt sauce (mix two tablespoons of plain yogurt, finely chopped mint, crushed garlic, and pepper).

Notes

Notes

Lunches

Pasta with eggplants, tomatoes, and feta cheese

- ◆ 3 servings
- ◆ 35 min
- ◆ 11 ingredients

Nutritional value per serving:
Calories: **767 kcal**
Proteins: **24 grams**
Fats: **3 grams**
Carbohydrates: **159 grams**

Ingredients:

- Pasta: 125 g
- Eggplants: 200 g
- Tomatoes: 125 g
- Red onion: 80 g
- Garlic: 5 g (1 clove)
- Feta cheese: 50 g

- Fresh parsley: 20 g
- Dried Italian herbs: 0.25 teaspoon
- Salt: to taste
- Ground black pepper: in pinch
- Olive oil: 30 ml (2 tablespoons)

Cooking instructions:

1. Prepare all the ingredients, including the red onion. You can use parsley, dill, celery, basil, or cilantro from the herbs.

2. Trim the edges of the eggplants and, if desired, remove the skin. Cut the eggplants into quarter rounds and transfer them to a deep bowl. Add a little salt and mix. Let them sit for 10 minutes to remove the bitterness. Then, squeeze the eggplants to remove the juice. In a deep skillet, heat the vegetable oil, add the eggplants, and sauté over medium heat, stirring, for 6-8 minutes until they develop a light golden crust.

3. Meanwhile, bring 1 liter of water to a boil in a pot and add a pinch of salt. Add the pasta to the boiling water and stir. Cook for 7-9 minutes after the water returns to a boil until almost done (1-2 minutes less than the time indicated on the package). Drain the cooked pasta in a colander.

4. Peel the onion and slice it into thin quarter rings. Add the onion to the eggplants and mix. Cook for 2-3 minutes over moderate heat, stirring. Cut the tomatoes into medium-sized pieces and add them to the other ingredients. Sauté everything for 2-4 minutes.

6. Add the cooked pasta to the vegetables.

5. Peel and mince the garlic, then add it to the skillet. Sprinkle in the ground black pepper, Italian herbs, and salt (keeping in mind the saltiness of the feta cheese). Mix well. Heat for 2-3 minutes over low heat.

6. Trim the stems from the parsley and finely chop the leaves. Crumble the feta cheese or cut it into small cubes. Add the parsley and feta cheese to the skillet.

7. Mix well. Heat for 1-2 minutes, then turn off the heat. The pasta with eggplants, tomatoes, and feta cheese is ready. Serve immediately

Cod with tomatoes

◆ 4 servings
◆ 15 min
◆ 7 ingredients

Nutritional value per serving:

Calories: **363 kcal**
Proteins: **37 grams**
Fats: **22 grams**
Carbohydrates: **5 grams**

Ingredients:

- Cod fillet: 0.8 kg
- Olive oil: 4 tablespoons
- Lemon: 1¼ pieces
- Parsley: 80 g
- Cherry tomatoes: 16 pieces
- Salt: to taste
- Ground black pepper: to taste

Cooking instructions:

1. Place one piece of cod in each, along with a tablespoon of chopped parsley, four halved cherry tomatoes, the juice of a quarter lemon, and a tablespoon of olive oil.

2. Seal the bag tightly, seasoning the contents with salt and pepper, and place it in an oven preheated to 350 degrees for fifteen minutes.

Baked fish in tomato sauce with feta cheese

◆ 4 servings
◆ 55 min
◆ 13 ingredients

Nutritional value per serving:

Calories: **253 kcal**
Proteins: **37 grams**
Fats: **10 grams**
Carbohydrates: **5 grams**

Ingredients:

- White fish fillet: 550 g
- Onion: 150 g
- Canned tomatoes in their own juice: 380 g
- Garlic: 2 cloves
- Feta cheese: 60 g
- Dry white wine: 30 ml (2 tablespoons)
- Dried oregano: 1 teaspoon
- Ground red pepper (hot): 1/4 teaspoon
- Ground black pepper: to taste
- Dried basil: 1 teaspoon
- Salt: to taste
- Olive oil: 20 ml (1 tablespoon)
- Fresh parsley: 2-3 sprigs

Cooking instructions:

1. Cut the fish fillet into portion-sized pieces. Place the fish in a baking dish in a single layer, season with salt (1/2 teaspoon) and pepper (1-2 pinches).

2. Peel the onion and garlic. Cut the onion into small cubes. Mince the garlic with a knife.

3. Heat the oil in a skillet. Add the onion and sauté over medium heat until soft, about 5 minutes.

4. Add the oregano and ground hot pepper. Mix well and sauté for 1 minute, then pour in the wine. Cook for 2 minutes.

5. Blend the peeled canned tomatoes in their juice until smooth. Pour the tomato puree into the skillet.

6. Simmer everything over medium heat without a lid for 10-15 minutes until the sauce thickens. Preheat the oven to 360 degrees. After some time, add the basil to the sauce.

7. Crumble the feta cheese into the sauce as well. Mix everything and season with salt to taste. Pour the sauce over the fish in the baking dish.

8. Place the dish in the preheated oven at 350 degrees and bake for about 20 minutes, until the fish is cooked through. Baked fish in tomato sauce with feta is ready. Garnish the dish with parsley.

Eggplants stewed with bell peppers and olives

♦ 4 servings
♦ 45 min
♦ 12 ingredients

Nutritional value per serving:
Calories: **380 kcal**
Proteins: **18 grams**
Fats: **10 grams**
Carbohydrates: **20 grams**

Ingredients:

- Eggplants: 450 g
- Onion: 300 g
- Bell pepper: 200 g
- Tomatoes: 250 g
- Olives (pitted): 70 g
- Garlic: 3 cloves
- Nutmeg: a pinch
- Ground red pepper (hot): 1-2 pinches
- Ground black pepper: to taste
- Salt: to taste
- Olive oil: 30 ml (2 tablespoons)
- Fresh basil: 15 g

Cooking instructions:

1. Peel the eggplants. Place the eggplants in a container and sprinkle with 0.5 teaspoon of salt. Let them sit for about 20 minutes. The eggplants will begin to release liquid. Peel the onion and cut it into wedges. Remove the seeds from the bell pepper and cut it into strips.

2. Add the onion to a skillet with heated olive oil. Sauté over low heat for 7-10 min until soft and lightly browned. Peel and mince the garlic with a knife, then add it to the onion. Stir and sauté for 40 sec.

3. Rinse the eggplants, dry them well, and cut them into small slices. Add the eggplants to the skillet and mix. Sauté for 5 minutes over medium-high heat.

4. Add the bell pepper to the skillet. Cut the tomatoes into small slices and add them to the skillet.

5. Slice the olives into rings and add them to the other ingredients. Sprinkle in salt, ground black and red pepper, and nutmeg.

6. Mix everything. Cover the skillet with a lid and simmer the contents over low heat for 5 min. Then remove the lid, increase the heat, and cook the eggplants with the peppers and olives for another 3-5 min to evaporate any excess liquid.

7. Chop the basil leaves and add them to the vegetables. Mix well and turn off the heat.

Rice with zucchini and spinach

◆ 3 servings
◆ 30 min
◆ 7 ingredients

Nutritional value per serving:
Calories: **350 kcal**
Proteins: **15 grams**
Fats: **12 grams**
Carbohydrates: **25 grams**

Ingredients:

• Long-grain rice (I have parboiled): 150 g
• Zucchini (young): 200 g (1 piece)
• Spinach: 50 g
• Celery (stalk): 1 piece
• Lemon (small): 70 g (0.5 piece)
• Salt: 0.5 teaspoon (to taste)
• Olive oil: 30 ml (2 tablespoons)

Cooking instructions:

1. Boil 1 liter of water in a pot or saucepan, add salt (0.5 teaspoons) to the water, and add the rice. Cook the rice over medium heat for 12-14 minutes or until done.

2. Trim the edges of the zucchini. Rinse the zucchini and the celery stalk. Cut the celery into small cubes and the zucchini into cubes about 0.8-1 cm on each side.

3. Heat the olive oil in a skillet, add the celery, and sauté for 1 minute until soft.

4. Add the zucchini and sauté together over medium heat, stirring, for 8-10 minutes.

5. Rinse the spinach, dry it, and cut it into strips. You can add the spinach once the zucchini and celery are soft and fragrant.

6. Add the spinach to the skillet, mix, and sauté for another 1 minute.

7. Season the contents of the skillet with a pinch of salt and squeeze in lemon juice to taste. Mix well.

8. Drain the rice in a colander or sieve to remove the water. Transfer the rice to the skillet with the zucchini, mix, and heat together with the vegetables and greens for another 2-3 minutes.

Notes

Spaghetti with shrimp and pistachios

- ◆ 4 servings
- ◆ 60 min
- ◆ 16 ingredients

Nutritional value per serving:

Calories: **628 kcal**
Proteins: **27 grams**
Fats: **28 grams**
Carbohydrates: **69 grams**

Ingredients:

- Spaghetti made from durum wheat: 450 g
- Green pistachios: 25 g
- Garlic: 2 cloves
- Fresh chili pepper: ½ piece
- Shrimp: 250 g
- Dry white wine: 50 ml
- Parsley: 10 g
- Olive oil: 50 ml
- Celery: 1 stalk
- Carrot: ½ piece
- Onion: ½ head
- Clove: ½ piece
- Butter: 10 g
- Tomato paste: 10 g
- Wheat flour: 5 g
- Salt: to taste

Cooking instructions:

1. Boil the shrimp in lightly salted water until done, peel off the shells, and set the shrimp aside. Place the shells in a small saucepan, add olive oil, and sauté with finely chopped onion, carrot, and celery for 5 minutes. Add roughly chopped garlic and tomato paste, and fry for another 1 minute. Pour in dry white wine, reduce the wine almost entirely, then add 1 liter of water or chicken broth, cloves, a pinch of salt, and simmer for about 20 minutes. Strain the mixture.

2. Mix about one-third of this liquid with 3 liters of water, add salt, boil, and cook the spaghetti in this liquid.

3. Heat the butter in sauté pan, fry the flour in it, then add the remaining shrimp broth. Cook, stirring, until the sauce thickens.

4. In the sauté pan, mix the sauce with the spaghetti, boiled shrimp, thinly sliced chili pepper, chopped pistachios, and minced herbs. Heat for 1 minute and serve.

Spaghetti with seafood and cherry tomatoes

◆ 2 servings
◆ 15 min
◆ 9 ingredients

Nutritional value per serving:
Calories: **343 kcal**
Proteins: **18 grams**
Fats: **11 grams**
Carbohydrates: **39 grams**

Ingredients:

• Spaghetti: 100 g
• Seafood cocktail: 150 g
• Cherry tomatoes: 8 pieces
• Olive oil: 1 tablespoon
• Red dry wine: to taste

• Basil: to taste
• Garlic: 1 clove
• Freshly ground black pepper: to taste
• Salt: to taste

Cooking instructions:

1. Cut the garlic clove in half. Similarly, cut each tomato into two halves. Heat the oil in a pan and add the garlic. Allow the oil to absorb its flavor, then add the tomatoes. Let them simmer on low heat until they become tender and slightly wrinkled. Remove the garlic.

2. Meanwhile, add the spaghetti to boiling water and cook until al dente.

3. Add the seafood to the tomatoes. If canned seafood is used in oil, let it drain; otherwise, the fish oil will overpower the olive oil's flavor. Without covering the pan, let the mixture cook on high heat to reduce, but be careful not to overcook. The octopus should have a golden crust.

4. Use a slotted spoon to scoop the pasta from the pot and add it to the seafood sauce. Pour in the wine and bring it to a boil. Sprinkle with dried basil.

Notes

Shrimp with rosemary

◆ 4 servings
◆ 15 min
◆ 9 ingredients

Nutritional value per serving:

Calories: **243 kcal**
Proteins: **12 grams**
Fats: **18 grams**
Carbohydrates: **5 grams**

Ingredients:

• Rosemary: 4 sprigs
• Shrimp: 12 pieces
• Olive oil: 50 ml
• Dry white wine: 100 ml
• Garlic: 6 cloves

• Butter: 20 g
• Chicken broth: 100 ml
• Ground black pepper: to taste
• Coarse salt: to taste

Cooking instructions:

1. Cut the large shrimp in half lengthwise along the back and remove the digestive tract.

2. Heat the olive oil in a large skillet and add the rosemary and shrimp. Sauté the shrimp on both sides until they turn pink, then add the garlic and cook until fragrant. Pour in the wine and chicken broth, adding a piece of butter to enrich the sauce. Season with salt and pepper, and simmer the shrimp for three to five minutes.

Notes

Mediterranean baked vege-table lasagna

- ◆ 4 servings
- ◆ 210 min
- ◆ 21 ingredients

Nutritional value per serving:
Calories: **409 kcal**
Proteins: **14 grams**
Fats: **27 grams**
Carbohydrates: **28 grams**

Ingredients:

- Eggplant: 1 piece
- Zucchini: 2 pieces
- Cherry tomatoes: 450 g
- Fresh red pepper: 1 piece
- Ready-made dry lasagna
- Sheets: 9 pieces
- Onion: 1 head
- Garlic: 2 cloves
- Basil leaves: to taste
- Olive oil: 2 tablespoons
- Pitted olives: 50 g

- Capers: 1 tablespoon
- Mozzarella cheese: 75 g
- Wheat flour: 35 g
- Butter: 40 g
- Milk: 570 ml
- Bay leaf: 1 piece
- Grated Parmesan cheese: tablespoons
- Nutmeg: to taste
- Salt: to taste
- Ground black pepper: to taste

Cooking instructions:

1. Cut the eggplant and zucchini into cubes. Mix with salt, transfer to a colander, cover with a plate, and place a weight on top. Let it sit for an hour to drain the liquid. Squeeze out any remaining moisture and pat dry with a towel. Peel the tomatoes, remove the seeds from the pepper, and chop both into cubes, along with the onion.

2. Place the tomatoes, eggplant, zucchini, pepper, and onion on a baking sheet, sprinkle with minced garlic and basil, and drizzle with olive oil. Mix everything thoroughly, season with salt and pepper, and bake at 350 degrees for 30–40 minutes until the edges of the vegetables are browned. Once cooked, sprinkle the roasted vegetables with chopped olives and capers.

3. For the sauce, mix flour, butter, and milk in a saucepan, adding the bay leaf, nutmeg, salt, and pepper to taste. Cook over medium heat, stirring constantly, until the sauce boils and thickens. Reduce the heat and cook for another 2 minutes. Stir in 3 tablespoons of grated Parmesan cheese. The sauce is ready.

4. Pour a quarter of the sauce into a baking dish and layer one-third of the vegetable mixture on top. Sprinkle with one-third of the grated mozzarella cheese and cover with a layer of lasagna sheets. Repeat the process, finishing with a layer of sauce. Sprinkle the remaining tablespoon of grated Parmesan cheese on top. Bake at 180 degrees for about 25–30 minutes until golden and crisp.

Pumpkin purée soup

- ◆ 4 servings
- ◆ 100 min
- ◆ 6 ingredients

Nutritional value per serving:

Calories: **327 kcal**
Proteins: **10 grams**
Fats: **17 grams**
Carbohydrates: **38 grams**

Ingredients:

- Pumpkin: 533 g
- Croutons: 100 g
- Water: 2 cups
- Potato: 200 g
- Water: 2 cups
- Milk: 3 cups
- Butter: 2 tablespoons
- Sugar: 1¼ teaspoons

Cooking instructions:

1. Peel the pumpkin and potato, wash them, and cut them into thin slices. Place them in a pot, cover with water, add salt, sugar, and a tablespoon of oil, then cook over low heat for 25-30 minutes.

2. Add the toasted or sautéed croutons, stir, and boil. Strain the mixture, pressing the remaining pulp through a sieve. Combine the strained mixture with hot milk (to the consistency of cream) and season with butter.

Potato and tuna casserole

◆ 4 servings
◆ 40 min
◆ 9 ingredients

Nutritional value per serving:

Calories: **243 kcal**
Proteins: **17 grams**
Fats: **5 grams**
Carbohydrates: **33 grams**

Ingredients:

• Canned tuna: 200 g
• Potatoes: 0.7 kg
• Onion: ¾ head
• Anchovies: 10 g
• Cream: 70 ml

• Gruyère cheese: 35 g
• Chopped parsley: 5 g
• Salt: to taste
• Ground black pepper: to taste

Cooking instructions:

1. Peel the potatoes and boil them in salted water until tender. Reserve some of the cooking water for the puree. Mash or pass the potatoes through a vegetable mill, add the cream, and whip with a whisk until smooth. If the puree is too thick, add some of the reserved broth. Season with salt and pepper to taste.

2. Slice the onion into thin half-rings and sauté in olive oil with chopped anchovies and thyme until caramelized. Combine the onions with the flaked tuna and finely chopped parsley. Season with black pepper.

3. Grease a large baking dish or several small ramekins with oil, layer the tuna mixture, and top with the mashed potatoes. Sprinkle with grated cheese and place in the oven for 15–20 minutes.

Notes

Chicken drumsticks with vegetables in sour cream sauce

◆ 4 servings
◆ 60 min
◆ 10 ingredients

Nutritional value per serving:

Calories: **465 kcal**
Proteins: **35 grams**
Fats: **15 grams**
Carbohydrates: **28 grams**

Ingredients:

- Chicken drumsticks: 4 pieces
- Young zucchini: 400 g
- Onion: 1½ pieces
- Tomatoes: 3¼ pieces
- Green string beans: 320 g
- Garlic: 2+1/2 cloves
- Ground black pepper: to taste
- Salt: to taste
- Mayonnaise: 1½ tablespoons
- 15% sour cream: 400 g

Cooking instructions:

1. Slightly sauté the chicken drumsticks in vegetable oil until halfway cooked, then remove them and set aside. In the same skillet, sauté the green string beans and onions for 10 minutes, then add the diced zucchini.

2. Mix the sour cream with the mayonnaise in a deep bowl, add the pepper mixture and garlic pressed through a garlic press. In a baking dish, layer the vegetable mixture, then place the chicken on top, followed by the tomatoes cut into large wedges.

3. Pour the sauce over the dish and spread it evenly. Bake for 20 minutes at 340 degrees 20 min.

Notes

Mediterranean tomato soup with squid

- ◆ 2 servings
- ◆ 30 min
- ◆ 14 ingredients

Nutritional value per serving:

Calories: **690 kcal**

Proteins: **31 grams**

Fats: **43 grams**

Carbohydrates: **41 grams**

Ingredients:

- Red onion: ½ head
- Garlic: 3 cloves
- Olive oil: 4 tablespoons
- Paprika: ½ teaspoon
- Dried oregano: ½ teaspoon
- Dry white wine: 50 ml
- Canned diced tomatoes: 500 g
- Lemon: ¼ piece
- Sugar: 2 teaspoons
- Ciabatta: 2 pieces
- Squid: 100 g
- Fresh basil: 2 sprigs
- Salt: to taste
- Ground black pepper: to taste

Cooking instructions:

1. Chop the red onion and garlic finely. If you need more instructions on preparing the Mediterranean Tomato Soup with Squid or further steps, let me know.

2. Sauté them in olive oil paprika and oregano until soft and lightly golden. Pour in the wine and let it reduce slightly.

3. After 30 sec, add the chopped tomatoes and 300 ml of water. Lower the heat and simmer the soup for 5 min. Season with salt and pepper, add lemon juice and sugar, then remove the soup from heat.

4. Toast the slices of bread in a toaster or dry fry them in a pan until golden brown.

5. Clean the squid by removing the quill and membranes, then slice them into rings. Heat olive oil in a pan and sauté the squid, stirring for 2–3 minutes.

6. Remove from heat, add chopped basil, and season with salt.

7. Pour the tomato soup into bowls, top with the squid and herbs, and serve with toasted bread.

Lentils in tomato sauce

◆ 4 servings
◆ 60 min
◆ 9 ingredients

Nutritional value per serving:
Calories: **322 kcal**
Proteins: **14 grams**
Fats: **14 grams**
Carbohydrates: **28 grams**

Ingredients:

• Green French lentils: 200 g

• Garlic: 4 cloves

• Water: 6 cups

• Extra virgin olive oil: 2 tablespoon

• Cherry tomatoes: 250 g

• Tomato sauce: 1 cup

• Sugar: 2 teaspoon

• Salt and black pepper: to taste

• Onion: 1 piece

Cooking instructions:

1. Start by preparing the lentils. Thinly slice the garlic and sauté it in 1 tablespoon of olive oil over low heat. Once it turns golden (not brown), add the lentils and pour in water with a pinch of salt. Bring to a boil, then reduce the heat to medium-low and cook for another 25 minutes, or until the lentils are tender yet still hold their shape.

2. For the tomato sauce, finely chop the onion and heat the remaining olive oil over medium heat. Sauté the onion until soft, then add the halved cherry tomatoes. Cook until the tomato juice turns the onion a light red color.

3. Add the tomato sauce, sugar, salt, and pepper. Simmer on low heat for 15–20 minutes, stirring occasionally. If the mixture begins to dry out, add some water as needed.

4. Stir the lentils into the tomato sauce, mixing everything well. Adjust the seasoning with salt and pepper to taste. Before serving, sprinkle some peeled sunflower seeds for added texture. This combination makes a hearty, flavorful dish, perfect as a standalone meal or a side.

Notes

Zucchini cream soup

- ◆ 4 servings
- ◆ 60 min
- ◆ 10 ingredients

Nutritional value per serving:

Calories: **252 kcal**

Proteins: **11 grams**

Fats: **8 grams**

Carbohydrates: **33 grams**

Ingredients:

- Olive oil: 40 ml
- Cream (20%): 135 ml
- Garlic: 1cloves
- Onion: 0,5 piece
- Potatoes: 1piece

- Carrot: 1 piece
- Zucchini: 2 pieces
- Chicken broth: 0.7 L
- White bread: 133 g
- Salt, pepper, herbs: to taste

Cooking instructions:

1. Peel and chop zucchini, potatoes, carrots, and onion. Heat vegetable oil in a pot and sauté the onion until it becomes translucent.

2. Add the garlic, crushed through a press, and sauté for half a minute. Add the zucchini, potatoes, and carrots to the pot. Sauté while stirring for about 7 minutes until the vegetables begin to soften.

3. Blend the soup until it reaches a smooth, creamy consistency.

4. Blend the soup using a blender until it reaches a smooth, creamy consistency.

5. Add the hot cream and broth to the soup until you reach the desired consistency. Season with salt and pepper to taste, and heat gently while stirring.

6. Cut the bread into large cubes and place them on a baking sheet. Sprinkle with salt and drizzle with oil. Bake in a preheated oven at (428°F) until golden brown, about 7–10 minutes. Serve the soup with croutons and your favorite herb.

Notes

Dubarry cream soup

- ◆ 4 servings
- ◆ 60 min
- ◆ 8 ingredients

Nutritional value per serving:

Calories: **328 kcal**
Proteins: **15 grams**
Fats: **19 grams**
Carbohydrates: **26 grams**

Ingredients:

- Cauliflower: piece
- Butter: 40 g
- Leek: 1 piece
- Chicken broth: 1 L
- Cream (35%): 100 ml
- Wheat flour: 40 g
- Salt: to taste
- Ground white pepper: to taste

Cooking instructions:

1. Chop the cauliflower, setting aside a dozen small, pretty florets.

2. Cut the white part of the leeks into random pieces.

3. Blanch the cauliflower florets in boiling water for 10 minutes, then transfer them to cold water to stop the cooking process.

4. In a deep saucepan, melt the butter and sauté the leeks over medium heat until soft. Be careful not to let the leeks change color, as this will affect the color of the soup.

5. Add the flour, mix well, remove the saucepan from the heat, and let the mixture cool for 10 min.

6. Pour the hot broth into the saucepan with the leeks and bring to a boil. Add the cauliflower and simmer on low heat for 20 minutes, until the cauliflower is tender.

7. Blend the soup until smooth, then add 75 ml of cream and boil, stirring with a wooden spoon. If the soup is too thick, gradually add 15 ml of cream, one tablespoon at a time, until the desired consistency is reached. Season with salt and pepper to taste.

8. Garnish the soup with the reserved cauliflower florets and fresh herbs when serving.

Eggplant purée soup

- ◆ 4 servings
- ◆ 30 min
- ◆ 8 ingredients

Nutritional value per serving:

Calories: **58 kcal**

Proteins: **3 grams**

Fats: **0 grams**

Carbohydrates: **12 grams**

Ingredients:

- Eggplants: 600 g
- Minced garlic: 2 cloves
- Chopped fresh thyme: to taste
- Olive oil: to taste
- Balsamic vinegar: 1 tablespoon
- Onion: 1 head
- Water: 500 ml
- Salt: to taste

Cooking instructions:

1. Peel the eggplants and cut them into half-round slices about 1 cm thick. Peel and mince the garlic, and slice the onion into thin half-rings. Remove the leaves from the thyme sprigs.

2. In a small skillet, heat olive oil over medium heat. Add the eggplant slices and thyme, then pour in the balsamic vinegar. Stir and add more olive oil. Sauté the eggplant slices until golden brown on all sides.

3. In a small skillet, heat olive oil over medium heat. Add the eggplant slices and thyme, then pour in the balsamic vinegar. Stir and add more olive oil. Sauté the eggplant slices until golden brown on all sides.

4. In a small pot, heat some olive oil and sauté the chopped onion and garlic over low heat until softened about seven to ten minutes. Add the sautéed eggplants, pour in water, and bring to a boil. Cover and simmer for twenty minutes.

5. Remove the pot from heat and use an immersion blender to puree the contents until smooth. You can strain the puree through a sieve if desired for a lighter texture. Add more water or broth as needed, and season with salt and pepper to taste. Garnish with any fresh herbs.

Sweet potato cream soup

♦ 2 servings
♦ 40 min
♦ 9 ingredients

Nutritional value per serving:
Calories: **322 kcal**
Proteins: **7 grams**
Fats: **16 grams**
Carbohydrates: **43 grams**

Ingredients:

• Sweet Potatoes: 2 pieces
• Carrot: 1 piece
• Leek: 1 piece
• Garlic: 2 cloves
• Fresh ginger: 5 g

• Salt: to taste
• Olive oil: 1 tablespoon
• Cold-pressed flaxseed oil: ½ tablespoon
• Flax seeds: 2 teaspoons

Cooking instructions:

1. Slice the leek into rings and sauté it in olive oil until softened.

2. Add the sweet potato and carrot, sliced into rings or diced into cubes. Stir and cook together with the leeks until they start to soften.

3. Add a small amount of water and simmer until the vegetables are tender.

4. Before the vegetables are fully cooked, add grated ginger to enhance the flavor.

5. Place the cooked sweet potatoes and carrots into a blender. Add crushed garlic and flaxseed oil, then blend until smooth to achieve a puréed consistency.

6. For added texture and flavor, serve the sweet potato purée with a garnish of flax seeds and garlic croutons.

Notes

Pea soup with bacon

◆ 4 servings
◆ 100 min
◆ 7 ingredients

Nutritional value per serving:
Calories: **390 kcal**
Proteins: **18 grams**
Fats: **17 grams**
Carbohydrates: **44 grams**

Ingredients:

• Potatoes: 3 pieces
• Mixed peas: 1 cup
• Bacon: 100 g
• Garlic: 1 clove

• Sunflower oil: 1 tablespoon
• Onion: 1 piece
• Salt and pepper: to taste

Cooking instructions:

1. Rinse the peas and transfer them to a pot. Add 1 liter of water, season with salt and pepper, bring to a boil, and then simmer for an hour with the lid on over low heat.

2. After an hour, add diced potatoes to the pot.

3. Finely chop the garlic and onion, then add them to a skillet. Sauté in sunflower oil until golden brown. Cut the bacon into strips about 1.5 to 2 centimeters wide and add it to the skillet with the onion and garlic. Fry until it reaches the desired level of crispiness.

4. Check if the potatoes are ready. If they are, mash the pea and potato mixture directly in the pot until smooth, then add the bacon along with the garlic and onion mixture. Stir everything together until well combined.

5. Stir the finished soup thoroughly, remove it from the heat, and let it rest for a bit. When serving, you can add a crispy bacon strip and some herbs on top for extra flavor and visual appeal.

Notes

Saint-Germain cream soup

- ◆ 4 servings
- ◆ 45 min
- ◆ 9 ingredients

Nutritional value per serving:

Calories: **225 kcal**
Proteins: **9 grams**
Fats: **14 grams**
Carbohydrates: **16 grams**

Ingredients:

- Green peas: 0.5 kg
- White part of leeks: 2 pieces
- Bacon: 100 g
- Butter: 2 tablespoons
- Meat broth: 2 cups
- Salt: to taste
- Sugar: 1 teaspoon
- Ground black pepper: a pinch
- Parsley: to taste

Cooking instructions:

1. Bring a pot of water to a boil, lightly salt it, and add the peas. Cook for 3 minutes after the water starts boiling, then drain them using a colander. Set aside half a cup of the peas in a separate dish.

2. Wash the leek cut it into thin rings, finely chop the bacon. Heat the butter in a pan sauté the leek until soft. Add the peas and pour in about one cup of broth. Simmer over low heat for 10–12 min.

3. Blend the cooked vegetables with the broth or pass them through a sieve until smooth.

4. Transfer the resulting puree into a separate pot, pour in the remaining broth, and add sugar, allspice, and salt to taste. Heat over medium heat for 5–7 minutes, stirring occasionally.

5. Add the green peas previously set aside. When serving, garnish with parsley leaves for a fresh touch and enhanced presentation.

Notes

Artichoke purée soup

◆ 4 servings
◆ 30 min
◆ 9 ingredients

Nutritional value per serving:

Calories: **864 kcal**
Proteins: **60 grams**
Fats: **48 grams**
Carbohydrates: **53 grams**

Ingredients:

• Beef: 1 kg
• Artichokes: 20 pieces
• Carrots: 2 pieces
• Butter: 50 g
• Wheat flour: 1 tablespoon

• Cream: ½ cup
• Egg yolk: 2 pieces
• Salt: to taste
• Ground black pepper: to taste

Cooking instructions:

1. Cook beef broth with root vegetables

2. Clean the artichokes, wash them, immerse them in boiling broth, cook until tender, and strain through a sieve.

3. Fry the flour in ½ tablespoon of oil, dilute with the broth, bring to a boil, and mix in the purée of artichokes.

4. Dilute the yolks and cream with a cup of broth, then gradually pour into the remaining broth while constantly stirring. Strain and bring to a boil.

5. Serve with croutons.

Notes

Corn cream soup

- ◆ 4 servings
- ◆ 30 min
- ◆ 8 ingredients

Nutritional value per serving:

Calories: **285 kcal**
Proteins: **20 grams**
Fats: **25 grams**
Carbohydrates: **73 grams**

Ingredients:

- Corn cobs: 1 piece
- Onion: 1 piece
- Celery root: 1 piece
- Wheat Flour: 3 tablespoons
- Butter: 40 g
- Milk: 1 L
- Vegetable Broth: 3 cups
- Corn flakes: to taste

Cooking instructions:

1. Chop the onion and sauté it. Add the corn kernels, celery, and sautéed onion to a small amount of boiling salted water, cover the pot with a lid, and simmer for 30–40 minutes.

2. The cooked vegetables are puréed, and a white sauce is prepared separately. The puréed corn is combined with the white sauce, diluted with broth or cooking liquid to the desired consistency, and brought to a boil. Then, boiling milk is added, and it is seasoned with butter.

3. Croutons or cornflakes are served with the soup.

Notes

Bean cream soup

- ◆ 4 servings
- ◆ 100 min
- ◆ 9 ingredients

Nutritional value per serving:

Calories: **529 kcal**

Proteins: **9 grams**

Fats: **38 grams**

Carbohydrates: **45 grams**

Ingredients:

- Onion: 2 pieces
- Beans: 3 cups
- Celery root: 1 piece
- Parsley root: 1 piece
- Carrots: 4 pieces

- Wheat flour: 6 tablespoons
- Olive oil: 0.8 cup
- Parsley: 40 g
- Water: 1,5 L

Cooking instructions:

1. The prepared beans are boiled. The diced onion, celery root, parsley root, and carrots are cooked until tender and then puréed.

2. The flour is sifted and sautéed in sunflower oil. Then diluted with the broth is diluted and combined with the puréed vegetables. Season with salt and cook for 4–5 minutes.

3. When serving, the soup is sprinkled with finely chopped parsley. Croutons are served with the soup.

Notes

Pepper cream soup

- ◆ 4 servings
- ◆ 20 min
- ◆ 8 ingredients

Nutritional value per serving:

Calories: **285 kcal**
Proteins: **20 grams**
Fats: **25 grams**
Carbohydrates: **73 grams**

Ingredients:

- Onion: 2 pieces
- Beans: 3 cups
- Celery root: 1 piece
- Parsley root: 1 piece
- Carrots: 4 pieces
- Wheat flour: 6 tablespoons
- Olive oil: 0.8 cup
- Parsley: 40 g
- Water: 1,5 L

- Fresh red peppers: 2 pieces
- Cucumbers: 2 pieces
- Olive oil: 50 ml
- Red onion: ½ head
- Salt: to taste
- Garlic: 2 cloves
- Cumin seeds: 1 teaspoon
- Water: 600 ml

Cooking instructions:

1. Roast the peppers in the oven at 400 degrees.

2. Sauté the onion and garlic until translucent.

3. Combine all the ingredients in a blender and blend quickly until creamy.

4. Season with pepper and salt. Garnish with flax seeds when serving. It can be served with sour cream and croutons.

Notes

Zucchini cream soup with cheese

◆ 4 servings
◆ 25 min
◆ 9 ingredients

Nutritional value per serving:

Calories: **324 kcal**
Proteins: **20 grams**
Fats: **10 grams**
Carbohydrates: **37 grams**

Ingredients:

- Zucchini: 2 pieces
- Carrot: 1¼ pieces
- Cauliflower: 167 g
- Onion: ¾ piece
- Herbs: to taste

- Croutons: to taste
- Salt: to taste
- Processed cheese: 2 pieces
- Ground black pepper: to taste

Cooking instructions:

1. Pour 2.5 liters of water into a pot and place it on the stove. While the water is heating, wash and peel the zucchini, carrots, and onion. Cut them into small pieces.

2. When the water boils, add all the vegetables to the pot, including the cauliflower (I usually use frozen). Reduce the heat by 2 notches and cook for 10 minutes.

3. Cut the processed cheese into small pieces, add it to the pot, and cook everything together for another 5 minutes. Season with salt and pepper.

4. Then, remove from the heat and blend everything with a blender until the vegetables and cheese are completely dissolved.

Notes

French broccoli and leek cream soup

- ◆ 4 servings
- ◆ 20 min
- ◆ 8 ingredients

Nutritional value per serving:

Calories: **124 kcal**
Proteins: **12 grams**
Fats: **9 grams**
Carbohydrates: **21 grams**

Ingredients:

- Broccoli: 0.5 kg
- Leek: 0.5 kg
- Garlic: 2 cloves
- Chicken eggs: 2 pieces
- Parsley: 1 bunch
- Salt: to taste
- Ground black pepper: to taste
- Cream: 200 ml

Cooking instructions:

1. Chop the broccoli and leeks, place them in water, boil them, and cook for 5–7 minutes. Strain the broth and let the vegetables cool.

2. Boil the eggs hard, then separate the yolks.

3. Blend the broccoli, leek, and parsley in a blender. Add them to the vegetable broth, place over low heat, and while stirring, add the cream. Then bring to a boil, add salt and pepper, and immediately remove from heat.

4. Grate the yolks and garlic until smooth. Add the mixture to the soup and gently stir.

Notes

Young pea cream soup

- ◆ 4 servings
- ◆ 20 min
- ◆ 10 ingredients

Nutritional value per serving:

Calories: **135 kcal**
Proteins: **5 grams**
Fats: **5 grams**
Carbohydrates: **20 grams**

Ingredients:

- Green peas: 250 g
- Potato: 150 g
- Vegetable broth: 500 ml
- Onion: 1 piece
- Garlic: 1 clove
- Natural yogurt: to taste
- Fresh mint: to taste
- Salt: to taste
- Ground black pepper: to taste
- Butter: 20 g

Cooking instructions:

1. Sauté the finely chopped garlic, onion, and diced potato in butter until golden brown, about 5–7 minutes, stirring constantly. Transfer to a pot with boiling broth. Reduce the heat, add the mint leaves, season with salt and pepper, and cook until the potatoes are tender.

2. Add the washed and peeled peas to the pot when the potatoes are ready and cook for 5–7 minutes. It's important not to overcook the peas, or they will lose their excellent color.

3. Transfer the soup to a blender or blend it with an immersion blender until smooth. Pour into bowls, add soft cheese or yogurt, and garnish with mint.

Notes

Spinach and seafood cream soup

◆ 4 servings
◆ 6 min
◆ 10 ingredients

Nutritional value per serving:
Calories: **302 kcal**
Proteins: **17 grams**
Fats: **21 grams**
Carbohydrates: **10 grams**

Ingredients:

• Celery stalk: 150 g

• Carrot: 150 g

• Spinach: 300 g

• Seafood cocktail: 500 g

• Garlic: 10 g

• Parsley: 50 g

• Onion: 200 g

• Spices: 10 g

• Cream (38%): 200 ml

• Olive oil: 50 ml

Cooking instructions:

1. Chop the celery, onion, and carrot randomly. Sauté in olive oil. Add water and simmer until tender. Finely chop the fresh spinach and add it to the vegetables. Blend and stir in the cream.

2. Cook for 5 minutes, adding the spices. Stir in the cream and blend until creamy.

3. Thaw the seafood, then place it in a heated skillet with olive oil and garlic.

4. Cut the toast bread into diamond, star, or other attractive shapes, and dry them in a toaster or oven. Place Parmesan cheese on top and bake in the oven.

5. Place the seafood cocktail in a deep plate, pour the soup over it, and garnish with croutons and herbs.

Notes

Asparagus cream soup

- ◆ 4 servings
- ◆ 35 min
- ◆ 5 ingredients

Nutritional value per serving:

Calories: **375 kcal**

Proteins: **11 grams**

Fats: **27 grams**

Carbohydrates: **22 grams**

Ingredients:

- White asparagus: 800 g
- Butter: 4 tablespoons
- flour: 2 tablespoons
- Milk: 4 cups
- Salt: to taste

Cooking instructions:

1. Select and clean 20-25 heads of asparagus for garnish. Wash the remaining asparagus, chop it, and boil it for 15-20 minutes with 2 cups of water and a little salt.

2. In a soup pot, lightly sauté two tablespoons of flour with the same amount of butter, then whisk in 4 cups of milk and bring to a boil. Add the asparagus (along with the cooking liquid) and simmer for 10-15 minutes. Then strain through a sieve and add salt to taste.

3. Before serving, stir in some butter and add the cooked asparagus for garnish to the soup. Serve the croutons separately.

Notes

Pureed chicken soup

- ◆ 4 servings
- ◆ 30 min
- ◆ 9 ingredients

Nutritional value per serving:

Calories: **322 kcal**
Proteins: **19 grams**
Fats: **24 grams**
Carbohydrates: **8 grams**

Ingredients:

- Chicken: 400 g
- Parsley: 50 g
- Carrot: 100 g
- Water: 1½ L
- Cream: 125 g

- Egg yolk: 2 pieces
- Wheat flour: 20 g
- Butter: 20 g
- Salt: to taste

Cooking instructions:

1. Prepare broth from chicken with vegetables and strain it. Separate the meat from the skin and bones, then pass it through a meat grinder.

2. Add the meat to the broth, thicken it with flour diluted in 100 g of cold water, bring it to a boil, and season it with salt to taste. Whisk the egg yolks with cream or sour cream, then pour them into the soup. Serve the soup with croutons.

Notes

Pureed tomato soup

- ◆ 4 servings
- ◆ 30 min
- ◆ 9 ingredients

Nutritional value per serving:

Calories: **171 kcal**

Proteins: **4 grams**

Fats: **12 grams**

Carbohydrates: **12 grams**

Ingredients:

- Carrot: 1 piece
- Canned tomatoes in their juice: 3 cans
- Onion: 1 head
- Basil: 1 bunch
- Garlic: 3 cloves
- 30% cream: 200 g
- Ground black pepper: to taste
- Salt: to taste
- Olive oil: to taste

Cooking instructions:

1. Remove the tomatoes from the pan and pour the juice they were canned in directly into the pot.

2. Chop the carrot and onion into small pieces, cutting them into thin slices resembling spaghetti, about 1–2 cm in width and length.

3. Sauté the carrot and onion in olive oil until golden brown.

4. Place the tomato juice over low heat.

5. Blend the tomatoes in a blender until smooth, ensuring no chunks.

6. When the tomato juice comes to a boil, add the puree from the blender, carrot, and onion. Cook for about 5 minutes.

7. Add the cream, stir, and bring to a boil. Before serving, garnish with basil. You can also add salted crackers.

Notes

Pureed liver soup

- ◆ 4 servings
- ◆ 60 min
- ◆ 9 ingredients

Nutritional value per serving:

Calories: **424 kcal**
Proteins: **19 grams**
Fats: **23 grams**
Carbohydrates: **26 grams**

Ingredients:

- Liver: 200 g
- Parsley root: 1 piece
- Carrot: 1 piece
- Onion: 2 heads
- Wheat flour: 6 tablespoons

- Butter: 80 g
- Milk: 1½ cups
- Chicken egg: 1 piece
- Vegetable broth: 1½ liters

Cooking instructions:

1. Lightly fry the liver, cut into pieces, together with the carrot and onion, then simmer until done with a small amount of broth. After that, puree the mixture, combine it with white sauce, season with salt, dilute with broth or water, and finish cooking.

2. Season the finished soup with boiled eggs.

Notes

Potato casserole

◆ 4 servings
◆ 30 min
◆ 5 ingredients

Nutritional value per serving:

Calories: **451 kcal**
Proteins: **12 grams**
Fats: **21 grams**
Carbohydrates: **57 grams**

Ingredients:

• Potatoes: 1 kg
• Onion: 3 heads
• Chicken eggs: 2 pieces

• Milk: 1 cup
• Butter: 3 tablespoons

Cooking instructions:

1. Boil the potatoes, then mash the hot cooked potatoes and add hot milk, raw eggs, salt, melted butter, and mix well.

2. Transfer half of the mashed potato mixture to a buttered pan and spread it evenly. Place a layer of sautéed onions on top, then cover with the remaining potato mixture and smooth it out. Brush with sour cream or drizzle with oil. Place in a hot oven and bake for 20-25 minutes. You can serve the casserole with milk, sour cream, or mushroom sauce.

Notes

Italian-style casserole

- ◆ 4 servings
- ◆ 60 min
- ◆ 7 ingredients

Nutritional value per serving:
Calories: **903 kcal**
Proteins: **68 grams**
Fats: **53 grams**
Carbohydrates: **41 grams**

Ingredients:

- Mashed potatoes: 1 kg
- Fresh mushrooms: 500 g
- Chicken breast fillet: 3 pieces
- Hard cheese: 350 g
- 30% cream: 150 ml
- Dill: 3 g
- Parsley: 3 g

Cooking instructions:

1. Peel and boil the potatoes.

2. Slice the mushrooms and chicken fillet, then sauté them.

3. For the sauce, mix the cream or milk with the seasonings, place over heat, and allow to warm up.

4. Grate the cheese using a coarse grater.

5. Finely chop the herbs.

6. Preheat the oven to 360 degrees.

7. Grease a baking sheet with oil, layer the potatoes on it, then add the chicken and mushrooms, pour the sauce over the top, and sprinkle with cheese.

8. Place the casserole in the oven for 15–20 minutes, until cooked through and the cheese is melted.

9. At the end of cooking, you can garnish with dill and parsley.

Notes

Zucchini casserole

- ◆ 4 servings
- ◆ 60 min
- ◆ 12 ingredients

Nutritional value per serving:

Calories: **300 kcal**
Proteins: **32 grams**
Fats: **14 grams**
Carbohydrates: **15 grams**

Ingredients:

- Chicken fillet: 400 g
- Sour cream: 60 g
- Dijon mustard: 15 g
- Onion: 100 g
- Vegetable oil: 15 ml
- Zucchini: 300 g
- Chicken eggs: 1½ pieces
- Wheat flour: 25 g
- Grated cheese: 50 g
- Lemon zest: to taste
- Salt: to taste
- Ground black pepper: to taste

Cooking instructions:

1. Chop the onion and fry it in vegetable oil until golden brown.

2. Grate the zucchini using a coarse grater, add a little salt, mix, and let it sit for 5–10 minutes, then squeeze out the juice.

3. Cut the chicken fillet into small cubes. Mix it with the zucchini and sautéed onions, then add the eggs. flour, mustard, sour cream, lemon zest, salt, and pepper.

4. Grease a baking dish with butter, spread the mixture evenly, and place it in an oven preheated to 360 degrees for 35 minutes.

5. Sprinkle the casserole with grated cheese, increase the temperature to 380degrees, and switch on the grill mode.

6. Bake the casserole until golden brown, about 5 minutes.

Notes

Chicken and zucchini casserole

- ◆ 4 servings
- ◆ 60 min
- ◆ 12 ingredients

Nutritional value per serving:

Calories: **258 kcal**
Proteins: **25 grams**
Fats: **14 grams**
Carbohydrates: **8 grams**

Ingredients:

- Chicken breast fillet: 1 piece
- Zucchini: ½ piece
- Cottage cheese: 100 g
- Chicken egg: 1 piece
- 20% cream: 50 ml
- Cheese: 100 g
- Wheat flour: 2 teaspoons
- Onion: ½ head
- Garlic: 1 clove
- Dried oregano: to taste
- Ground black pepper: to taste
- Salt: to taste

Cooking instructions:

1. Preheat the oven to 360 degrees Fahrenheit. Boil the chicken fillet in salted water. It doesn't need to cook for long; it should remain juicy. Cut the fillet into pieces and set aside to cool.

2. Slice the onion into half rings and fry it in vegetable oil until golden brown.

3. Coarsely chop more than half of the zucchini, add it to the onion, and sauté until soft. Mince the garlic and add it to the vegetables.

4. Grate the cheese using a coarse grater. Whisk the eggs with a pinch of salt. Mix the beaten eggs, half cheese, flour, cream, and cottage cheese. Add the chicken fillet and the zucchini with onion and garlic, season with salt, and mix everything well once more.

5. Next, pour the batter into a mold, preferably a springform pan, as it's more convenient. Add pepper and sprinkle with oregano. Slice the remaining zucchini thinly and arrange it on top of the batter. Then, sprinkle the top layer with the remaining grated cheese and bake for 30–40 minutes, until the cheese on top is golden brown.

Meat casserole

- ◆ 4 servings
- ◆ 60 min
- ◆ 15 ingredients

Nutritional value per serving:

Calories: **424 kcal**

Proteins: **21 grams**

Fats: **28 grams**

Carbohydrates: **31 grams**

Ingredients:

- Potatoes: 0.5 kg
- Ground beef: 250 g
- Onion: ½ head
- Carrot: ½ piece
- Canned diced tomatoes: 200 g
- Frozen green peas: 50 g
- Parsley: 15 g
- Chicken egg: ½ piece
- Butter: 25 g
- Hard cheese: 75 g
- Vegetable oil: 15 ml
- Salt: to taste
- Ground black pepper: to taste
- Nutmeg: to taste
- Breadcrumbs: 8 g

Cooking instructions:

1. Peel the potatoes; if they are large, cut them into 2–4 pieces, cover with water, and boil until tender.

2. When the potatoes are ready, drain the water, add the butter, and mash into a puree. Season with salt and add nutmeg to taste, along with 100 grams of grated cheese and the egg. Mix well.

3. Chop the onion into small cubes and cut the carrot into cubes about 1 cm on each side.

4. Heat vegetable oil in a skillet and sauté the onion until golden brown. Add the carrot to the onion and sauté, stirring, for another 5 minutes. Add the ground beef to the skillet and cook, stirring, until the meat changes color completely. Add the canned tomatoes to the skillet, mix well, and simmer until all the liquid evaporates, about 10–15 minutes.

5. Spread the meat mixture in a baking dish. Spread the mashed potatoes on top and smooth them out. Sprinkle with the remaining grated cheese and place in an oven preheated to 400 degrees.

6. Bake the dish in the oven for about 20–25 minutes, until the top layer turns golden brown.

7. After cooking, let the casserole cool slightly, about 5–10 minutes, to make it easier to slice.

8. Cut into portions and serve, optionally garnishing with fresh herbs such as parsley or thyme.

Fish casserole

- ◆ 2 servings
- ◆ 30 min
- ◆ 6 ingredients

Nutritional value per serving:

Calories: **522 kcal**
Proteins: **48 grams**
Fats: **26 grams**
Carbohydrates: **1 grams**

Ingredients:

- Cod fillet: 400 g
- Butter: 2 tablespoons
- Lemon: ½ piece
- Cheese: 100 g
- Ground black pepper: to taste
- Salt: to taste

Cooking instructions:

1. Pass the fish fillet through a meat grinder, and grate the cheese on a fine grater. Mix the minced fish with the cheese, one tablespoon of butter, lemon juice, and season with salt and pepper.

2. Spread the entire mixture onto a greased skillet and bake in the oven.

3. Bake in a preheated oven at 180°C (350°F) for about 20–25 minutes, until the top becomes golden and slightly browned.

4. After baking, let the dish cool slightly, then carefully slice into portions.

5. Serve hot, optionally garnishing with fresh herbs.

Notes

Turkey casserole

◆ 4 servings
◆ 30 min
◆ 11 ingredients

Nutritional value per serving:

Calories: **211 kcal**
Proteins: **17 grams**
Fats: **6 grams**
Carbohydrates: **22 grams**

Ingredients:

• Turkey fillet: 200 g
• Potatoes: 3¼ pieces
• Carrot: 1¼ pieces
• Onion: ¾ piece
• Bell pepper: 1¼ pieces
• Chicken egg: ¾ piece

• Sour cream: 27 g
• Feta cheese: 67 g
• Mint: to taste
• Salt: to taste
• Ground black pepper: a pinch

Cooking instructions:

1. Grate the carrot and potato on a coarse grater. Cut the onion into half rings.

2. Sauté everything until half cooked.

3. Pass the meat through a meat grinder (you can use pre-made ground meat), add it to the vegetables, and cook for another 10 min. Add mint (fresh or dried), and season with salt and pepper to taste.

4. Finely chop the bell pepper, add it to the vegetables, and sauté for another 5 minutes.

5. Beat the egg, sour cream, and feta cheese with a mixer in a deep bowl (if the feta cheese is hard, soak it in boiling water for about 10 minutes first.

6. Place the vegetables in a baking dish, pour the beaten sauce over them, and bake in an oven at 360 degrees until golden brown.

Notes

Irish stew

- ◆ 4 servings
- ◆ 120 min
- ◆ 9 ingredients

Nutritional value per serving:

Calories: **905 kcal**
Proteins: **45 grams**
Fats: **63 grams**
Carbohydrates: **44 grams**

Ingredients:

- Any meat fillet: 1 kg
- Potatoes: 10 pieces
- Onion: 3 pieces
- Garlic: 6 cloves
- Carrots: 4 pieces

- Parsley: 4 sprigs
- Salt: to taste
- Fresh rosemary: 1 sprigs
- Boiling water: 600 ml

Cooking instructions:

1. Peel and chop the vegetables into large pieces. Cut the meat in the same way, season with salt, and fry in heated oil for 3 minutes on each side. Add the onion, garlic, carrot, and rosemary leaves. Cook, stirring, for 5 minutes.

2. Pour in the boiling water, stir, and bring to a boil. Season to taste. Reduce the heat, add the potatoes, and cook covered for 2 hours.

3. Add 3–4 ice cubes and skim off the fat that has risen to the surface with a spoon. Bring to a boil once more, add the chopped herbs, and serve on plates.

Notes

Tuna stew

♦ 4 servings
♦ 30 min
♦ 12 ingredients

Nutritional value per serving:
Calories: **248 kcal**
Proteins: **20 grams**
Fats: **11 grams**
Carbohydrates: **14 grams**

Ingredients:

- Tuna fillet: 300 g
- Onion: 1 piece
- Garlic: 1 clove
- Orange: 1 piece
- Red wine: 100 ml
- Olive oil: 2 tablespoons
- Tomato paste: 1 tablespoon
- Cinnamon stick: 1 piece
- Mixed salad leaves: 150 g
- Fresh bay leaves: 3 pieces
- Breadcrumbs: 10 g
- Salt: to taste

Cooking instructions:

1. Finely chop the onion, garlic, and orange zest, and toss them into a heated pan with olive oil. Add the bay leaves and cinnamon, and sauté for five to ten minutes.

2. Add the tuna fillet (whole or cut into pieces) to the pan, season with salt and pepper to taste, sear on all sides, then remove from the pan.

3. Pour the red wine into the pan and add the tomato paste. Let the wine. Reduce, then add the tuna, cut into pieces, and warm it up. Before serving, sprinkle with toasted breadcrumbs and garnish with mixed salad leaves and orange zest.

4. Pour red table wine into the pan and add the tomato paste. Let the wine evaporate, then add the tuna, cut into pieces, and warm it up. Before serving, sprinkle with toasted breadcrumbs and garnish with mixed salad leaves and orange zest.

Notes

Seafood stew

- ◆ 4 servings
- ◆ 60 min
- ◆ 20 ingredients

Nutritional value per serving:
Calories: **248 kcal**
Proteins: **20 grams**
Fats: **11 grams**
Carbohydrates: **14 grams**

Ingredients:

- Fish broth: 200 ml
- Dry white wine: 230 ml
- Scallops: 120 g
- Dried olives: 4 g
- Cilantro: 12 g
- Conger eel fillet: 440 g
- Tiger prawns: 400 g
- Green oil: 12 g
- Mussels: 340 g
- Parsley: 8 g
- Tomatoes concassed: 240 g
- Cream: 160 ml
- Garlic: 95 g
- Vegetable oil: 30 ml
- Water: 1.30 L
- Thyme: 2 sprigs
- Tomatoes: 140 g
- Onion: 110 g
- Carrot: 150 g
- Celery stalk: 65 g

Cooking instructions:

1. First, prepare the bisque. Chop the celery, carrots, onion, and tomatoes. Peel the shrimp. Sauté the vegetables with the shrimp shells, thyme, and garlic, then pour in 110 ml of white wine. Blend the mixture, strain it through a sieve, pour in water, and bring to a boil.

2. Finely chop the garlic and cilantro. Cut the fish into 5 cm pieces, the scallops into 2x2 cm cubes, and the tomatoes concussed into 3x3 cm cubes. Salt and mix all the seafood.

3. Pour oil into a heated skillet, add 80 g of garlic, and sauté for one minute until fragrant. Then add the tomatoes and sauté for another 20 sec. Add the shrimp and mussels, and sauté for 2 min. Pour in 120 ml of white wine and let it evaporate. Then add the fish broth and reduce it by half.

4. Add the conger eel and reduce the broth again.

5. Pour in the cream, add 80 g of tomatoes and parsley, and heat for 1–2 min. Add the scallops and bisque, stir over high heat, and serve in a deep plate. Garnish with black olives, the remaining tomatoes, sprigs of cilantro, and drops of green oil.

Notes

Salads

Vegetable salad with seafood

◆ 4 servings
◆ 20 min
◆ 7 ingredients

Nutritional value per serving:

Calories: **270 kcal**
Proteins: **21 grams**
Fats: **16 grams**
Carbohydrates: **8 grams**

Ingredients:

• Green salad: 1 bunch

• Tomatoes: 6 pieces

• Olive oil: 55 ml

• Lemon: ½ piece

• Salt: to taste

• Ground black pepper: to taste

• Seafood cocktail: 500 g

Cooking instructions:

1. Bring water to a boil in a pot, then add the seafood cocktail. Cook for 5–7 minutes. Then, drain the seafood in a colander and rinse with cold water.

2. Then, cut the tomatoes into cubes and the lettuce leaves. Combine everything with the seafood in a salad bowl and mix well.

3. Dress the salad with olive oil, squeeze in lemon juice, and season with salt and pepper to taste.

Notes

Vegetable salad with couscous

- ◆ 4 servings
- ◆ 20 min
- ◆ 11 ingredients

Nutritional value per serving:

Calories: **270 kcal**

Proteins: **21 grams**

Fats: **16 grams**

Carbohydrates: **8 grams**

Ingredients:

- Couscous: 200 g
- Red bell pepper: 1 piece
- Yellow bell pepper: 1 piece
- Green onion: 1 bunch
- Fresh mint: 7 g
- Spices: to taste
- Parsley: to taste
- Red wine vinegar: 1 tablespoon
- Sea salt: to taste
- Ground black pepper: to taste
- Vegetable oil: 2 tablespoons

Cooking instructions:

1. Cook the couscous according to the instructions on the package.

2. Wash the peppers, remove the seeds and stems, and cut them into cubes. Chop the onion and parsley.

3. Combine the couscous, vegetables, herbs, oil, and wine vinegar in a large bowl. Season with salt and pepper, add spices to taste and garnish the dish with fresh mint.

Notes

Fresh Vegetable Salad

- ◆ 2 servings
- ◆ 15 min
- ◆ 14 ingredients

Nutritional value per serving:

Calories: **600 kcal**

Proteins: **7 grams**

Fats: **51 grams**

Carbohydrates: **28 grams**

Ingredients:

- Fresh red bell pepper: ½ piece
- Mixed salad leaves: 100 g
- Ground white pepper: to taste
- Cherry tomatoes: 6 pieces
- Shallot onion: 1 head
- Ginger root: 1 piece
- Cucumber: ½ piece

- Garlic: 1 clove
- Rice vinegar: 1½ tablespoons
- Ketchup: 1 tablespoon
- Water: 1 tablespoon
- Light soy sauce: 3 tablespoons
- Vegetable oil: 100 ml
- Salt: to taste

Cooking instructions:

1. In a small bowl, mix the chopped shallot, grated ginger, minced garlic, rice vinegar, ketchup, water, vegetable oil, and soy sauce.

2. Remove the seeds from the pepper and cut it into thin strips. Place it in ice water for a while until the pieces curl up. This will take a few minutes.

3. Place the salad leaves and mix with 4-6 tablespoons of the dressing. Season with salt. Divide the salad between 2 plates, and top with halved cherry tomatoes, thinly sliced cucumber, and strips of pepper.

Notes

Vegetable Salad with Eggplants

◆ 2 servings
◆ 20 min
◆ 11 ingredients

Nutritional value per serving:

Calories: **835 kcal**
Proteins: **7 grams**
Fats: **84 grams**
Carbohydrates: **14 grams**

Ingredients:

• Eggplant: 1 piece
• Cucumbers: 2 pieces
• Watercress: 1 bunch
• Cilantro: 1 bunch
• Parsley: 1 bunch
• Mustard oil: 8 tablespoons

• Sour cream: 4 tablespoons
• Dijon mustard: 2 teaspoons
• Cherry tomatoes: 8 pieces
• Sesame seeds: 2 teaspoons
• Sea salt: to taste

Cooking instructions:

1. Cut the eggplant into small cubes.

2. Place the eggplant in heated mustard oil in a skillet after soaking them in salted water.

3. Season with salt and stir. Sauté over high heat for 6–7 minutes, stirring occasionally. Then transfer to a serving dish.

4. Peel the cucumber and cut it into small pieces. Season with salt.

5. In a deep bowl, mix the mustard and sour cream.

6. Mix the eggplant into the resulting sauce. Add the cucumber.

7. Finely chop the herbs. Add it to the salad and sprinkle with sesame seeds. Mix well.

8. Cut the tomatoes into 3–4 pieces. Add them to the salad and serve.

Notes

Vegetable salad with shrimp

- ◆ 2 servings
- ◆ 15 min
- ◆ 5 ingredients

Nutritional value per serving:

Calories: **185 kcal**
Proteins: **24 grams**
Fats: **8 grams**
Carbohydrates: **14 grams**

Ingredients:

- Peeled cooked shrimp: 500 g
- Tomatoes: 3 pieces
- Olive oil: 20 ml
- Cucumbers: 2 pieces
- Salt: to taste

Cooking instructions:

1. Cut the tomatoes and cucumbers into cubes.

2. Combine everything with the shrimp. Add salt to taste and dress with olive oil.

Notes

Vegetable salad with meat

◆ 4 servings
◆ 20 min
◆ 9 ingredients

Nutritional value per serving:
Calories: **282 kcal**
Proteins: **13 grams**
Fats: **20 grams**
Carbohydrates: **14 grams**

Ingredients:

• Tomatoes: 2 pieces
• Iceberg lettuce: 1 head
• Chicken eggs: 3 pieces
• Cheese: 100 g
• Garlic: 3 cloves

• Mayonnaise: 3 tablespoons
• Croutons: ½ cup
• Any meat: 150 g
• Avocado: 1 piece

Cooking instructions:

1. Cut the iceberg lettuce into thin strips, and dice the tomatoes, eggs, and meat into cube.

2. Mix and dress with mayonnaise and garlic. Add salt to taste. Stir well.

3. Grate the cheese on a fine grater and add it to the salad.

4. Slice the avocado and add it to the salad.

5. Garnish with croutons before serving.

Notes

Vegetable salad with cheese and salmon

◆ 4 servings
◆ 15 min
◆ 10 ingredients

Nutritional value per serving:

Calories: **451 kcal**
Proteins: **20 grams**
Fats: **36 grams**
Carbohydrates: **9 grams**

Ingredients:

- Chinese cabbage: 65 g
- Avocado: 1 piece
- Extra virgin olive oil: 2 tablespoons
- Grated Parmesan cheese: 1½ tablespoons
- Salmon: 85 g
- Lemon: 1 piece
- Sun-dried tomatoes: 3 pieces
- Quail eggs: 4 pieces
- Ground black pepper: to taste
- Saffron: to taste

Cooking instructions:

1. Chop the green parts of the Chinese cabbage into small pieces.

2. Add the diced avocado and dress with olive oil.

3. Add salt and season with saffron.

4. Top with cheese and chili pepper.

5. Shred the salmon and place it in a skillet, seasoning with black pepper. Drizzle with lemon juice.

6. Sauté for about 3–4 minutes over high heat, stirring occasionally. Then allow to cool slightly.

7. Dice the tomatoes. Add the tomatoes to the other ingredients.

8. Then add the quarters of the hard-boiled quail eggs.

9. Place the fish on top and serve.

Notes

Bean salad

- ◆ 4 servings
- ◆ 25 min
- ◆ 13 ingredients

Nutritional value per serving:
Calories: **372 kcal**
Proteins: **15 grams**
Fats: **24 grams**
Carbohydrates: **25 grams**

Ingredients:

- Canned white beans: 1 can
- Cucumbers: 2 pieces
- Red onion: ½ head
- Cherry tomatoes: 300 g
- Kalamata olives: 70 g
- Parsley: 20 g
- Olive oil: 50 ml
- Garlic: 1 clove
- Lemon: ½ piece
- Salt: to taste
- Sugar: to taste
- Ground black pepper: to taste
- Feta cheese: 150 g

Cooking instructions:

1. For the dressing, mix olive oil, lemon juice, crushed garlic, salt, pepper, and sugar in a bowl until well combined.

2. Rinse the canned beans and let them drain in a colander to remove excess liquid.

3. Dice the red onion and cucumbers into small cubes.

4. Pit the olives and chop them coarsely.

5. Cut the cherry tomatoes in half.

6. Crumble the feta cheese with a fork until it forms curd-like chunks.

7. Chop the parsley, removing the stems.

8. In a large bowl, combine all the prepared ingredients, drizzle the salad with the dressing, and serve immediately.

Protein salad with quinoa and beans

◆ 4 servings
◆ 10 min
◆ 13 ingredients

Nutritional value per serving:
Calories: **150 kcal**
Proteins: **8 grams**
Fats: **5 grams**
Carbohydrates: **15 grams**

Ingredients:

• Lemon juice: 65 ml
• Garlic: 1 clove
• Cilantro (coriander): 56 g
• Ground cumin: 1 teaspoon
• Olive oil: 50 ml
• Quinoa: ½ cup
• Canned red beans: 185 g

• Canned corn: 185 g
• Sweet pepper: 1¾ pieces
• Chili pepper: 1 piece
• Green onions: 28 g
• Salt: to taste
• Ground black pepper: to taste

Cooking instructions:

1. Mix lemon juice, salt, crushed garlic, half of the chopped cilantro, and cumin in a small bowl, then pour in the oil. Add pepper to taste. Set aside.

2. Rinse the quinoa under running water in a sieve until the water runs clear. Bring water to a boil, add salt, and cook the quinoa for 15 minutes. Drain the cooked quinoa in a sieve.

3. Remove the seeds from the sweet pepper and dice it into small cubes.

4. Remove the seeds from the chili pepper and chop it finely. Chop the cilantro and green onions.

5. Combine the beans, corn, vegetables, herbs, and cooled quinoa in a large bowl. Gently toss with the dressing.

Notes

Salad with pita

- ◆ 2 servings
- ◆ 30 min
- ◆ 13 ingredients

Nutritional value per serving:

Calories: **644 kcal**
Proteins: **10 grams**
Fats: **38 grams**
Carbohydrates: **63 grams**

Ingredients:

- Tomatoes: 2 pieces
- Green onions: 4 pieces
- Cucumber: 1 piece
- Red onion: 1 piece
- Sweet pepper: 3 pieces
- Chopped parsley: 6 tablespoons
- Fresh mint: 2 tablespoons
- Olive oil: 150 ml
- Lemon zest: 1 piece
- Salt: to taste
- Ground black pepper: to taste

Cooking instructions:

1. Place the herbs and chopped vegetables in a large container and mix thoroughly.

2. In a separate container, whisk together the dressing ingredients, adding salt and pepper to taste.

3. Pour the dressing over the salad and mix again.

4. Pour the dressing over the salad and mix again.

5. Mix the mixture, stuff it into the pita, and serve immediately.

Notes

Salad with lightly salted salmon

◆ 2 servings
◆ 10 min
◆ 12 ingredients

Nutritional value per serving:
Calories: **439 kcal**
Proteins: **16 grams**
Fats: **41 grams**
Carbohydrates: **4 grams**

Ingredients:

- Arugula: 30 g
- Avocado: ½ piece
- Cherry tomatoes: 60 g
- Lightly salted salmon: 120 g
- Extra virgin olive oil: 3 tablespoons
- White wine vinegar: 1 teaspoon
- Lemon juice: 1 teaspoon
- Dried basil: 1 teaspoon
- Ground black pepper: to taste
- Sea salt: to taste
- White sesame seeds: ½ teaspoon
- Sesame seeds: ½ teaspoon

Cooking instructions:

1. Place the arugula on a plate.

2. Peel and slice the avocado. Drizzle the avocado with lemon juice. Add salt to taste.

3. Place the avocado on top of the arugula.

4. Cut the salmon into cubes.

5. Add the salmon to the salad.

6. Cut the cherry tomatoes in half.

7. Add the tomatoes to the salad.

8. In a small bowl, mix the oil and wine vinegar. Add the sesame seeds.

9. Add dried red basil and pepper to taste.

10. Mix the dressing thoroughly. Drizzle the salad with the dressing and serve.

Classic caesar salad with chicken and mustard dressing

◆ 4 servings
◆ 60 min
◆ 14 ingredients

Nutritional value per serving:

Calories: **726 kcal**
Proteins: **44 grams**
Fats: **52 grams**
Carbohydrates: **14 grams**

Ingredients:

- Mixed salad greens: ½ bunch
- Tomatoes: 5 pieces
- White bread: ½ piece
- Chinese cabbage: ½ piece
- Garlic: 2 cloves
- Chicken fillet: 400 g
- Olive oil: 150 ml

- Chicken eggs: 6 pieces
- Table mustard: 4 tablespoons
- Egg yolks: 4 pieces
- Apple cider vinegar: 1 tablespoon
- Salt: to taste
- Ground black pepper: to taste
- Anchovies: 20 g

Cooking instructions:

1. Cut the chicken fillet into medium-sized pieces and sauté. Tear the salad leaves and Chinese cabbage by hand and chop the tomatoes and eggs coarsely.

2. Cut the white bread into large cubes (1.5x1.5 cm), place them in an ungreased skillet, and toast until dry on medium heat.

3. Finely chop the garlic and sauté it in olive oil (3–4 tablespoons) until golden. Later, drizzle this dressing evenly over the croutons.

4. Mustard dressing: four egg yolks, four tablespoons of mustard, one tablespoon of apple cider vinegar: add salt and pepper, and whisk with a mixer until smooth. While continuing to whisk, gradually pour in olive oil (the amount depends on the desired consistency). Add the anchovies and whisk again.

Notes

Salad with spinach, sun-dried tomatoes, and chickpeas

- ◆ 4 servings
- ◆ 10 min
- ◆ 6 ingredients

Nutritional value per serving:

Calories: **599 kcal**
Proteins: **22 grams**
Fats: **27 grams**
Carbohydrates: **69 grams**

Ingredients:

- Fresh spinach: 1 bunch
- Sun-dried tomatoes in oil: 200 g
- Large pitted olives: 200 g
- Canned chickpeas: 200 g
- Olive oil: 1 tablespoon
- Balsamic vinegar: 1 teaspoon

Cooking instructions:

1. Rinse the spinach leaves and dry them.

2. Add the sun-dried tomatoes.

3. Cut the large green olives in half.

4. Add the canned chickpeas.

5. Use olive oil and balsamic vinegar as the dressing.

Notes

Salad with shrimp, melon, watermelon, and arugula

- ◆ 4 servings
- ◆ 20 min
- ◆ 10 ingredients

Nutritional value per serving:
Calories: **284 kcal**
Proteins: **13 grams**
Fats: **21 grams**
Carbohydrates: **11 grams**

Ingredients:

- Tiger shrimp: 6 pieces
- Arugula: 67 g
- Watermelon: 133 g
- Melon: 133 g
- Dill: 13 g

- Olive oil: 80 ml
- Balsamic vinegar: 27 ml
- Honey: 2 tablespoons
- Salt: to taste
- Ground black pepper: to taste

Cooking instructions:

1. Soak the arugula in cold water and let it sit for 10 minutes.

2. Peel the shrimp, finely chop the dill, and mix the shrimp with the dill and 50 ml of oil. Add salt.

3. Cut the watermelon and melon into random shapes.

4. Mix 70 ml of oil, balsamic vinegar, honey, and salt.

5. Sauté the shrimp in a small amount of olive oil for 1.5 minutes on one side, then flip and cook for another 30 seconds.

6. Drain the arugula in a sieve or lift it out of the water with your hands, but do not squeeze it. Place the arugula on a plate, top with pieces of watermelon and melon, and add the shrimp, and generously drizzle with the balsamic dressing.

Notes

Salad with octopus

◆ 2 servings
◆ 30 min
◆ 5 ingredients

Nutritional value per serving:

Calories: **244 kcal**
Proteins: **29 grams**
Fats: **10 grams**
Carbohydrates: **8 grams**

Ingredients:

• Octopus: 300 g
• Sweet red onion: ½ piece
• Tomatoes: 250 g

• Olive oil: 1 tablespoon
• Vinegar: 1 tablespoon

Cooking instructions:

1. First, finely chop the onion and scald it with boiling water. This simple procedure will remove the bitterness from the onion. Drain the boiling water and pour a tablespoon of vinegar over the onion.

2. Boil water for the octopus (add lemon, salt, pepper, rosemary, and anything else you like with seafood).

3. Place the octopus in the pot as soon as the water boils, and cook until done. Mine were small, so I cooked them for three minutes.

4. Cut the tomatoes into small pieces. Add herbs to them (I added basil, parsley, and cilantro.

5. Take out the octopus and cut them into pieces.

6. Mix all the ingredients and dress the salad with salt, pepper, olive oil, and balsamic vinegar.

Notes

Potato salad without mayonnaise

◆ 4 servings
◆ 60 min
◆ 9 ingredients

Nutritional value per serving:
Calories: **190 kcal**
Proteins: **4 grams**
Fats: **6 grams**
Carbohydrates: **31 grams**

Ingredients:

• Potatoes: 6 pieces
• Green onions: 4 stalks
• Gherkins: 60 g
• Whole grain mustard: 1 tablespoon
• Vinegar: ¼ cup

• Olive oil: 1 tablespoon
• Sugar: 1 teaspoon
• Salt: ¼ teaspoon
• Ground black pepper: ¼ teaspoon

Cooking instructions:

1. Peel and chop the potatoes. Transfer them to a pan and cover with water, ensuring it completely covers the potatoes. Then bring to a boil. Reduce the heat and cook until tender, about 20 minutes. Drain the water and rinse the potatoes under cold running water to cool.

2. In a large bowl, whisk together the mustard, vinegar, olive oil, salt, and pepper.

3. Add the cooled potatoes, green onions, and gherkins.

4. Mix well and refrigerate until serving time.

Notes

Italian salad with ham, cheese, and vegetables

◆ 4 servings
◆ 30 min
◆ 7 ingredients

Nutritional value per serving:

Calories: **650 kcal**
Proteins: **33 grams**
Fats: **28 grams**
Carbohydrates: **87 grams**

Ingredients:

• Ham: 300 g
• Tomatoes: 2 pieces
• Sweet peppers: 2 pieces
• Pasta: 400 g
• Canned corn: 300 g
• Cheese: 200 g
• Mustard: to tasty
• Sour cream: to tasty

Cooking instructions:

1. Boil the pasta — it's best to use shaped pasta made from durum wheat — in salted water, drain, and let it cool.

2. Dice the tomatoes and peppers, slice the ham into thin pieces, and grate the cheese on a coarse grater.

3. Mix all the ingredients and dress the salad with mayonnaise.

Notes

Salad with duck breast, arugula, and cranberry sauce

- ◆ 4 servings
- ◆ 30 min
- ◆ 15 ingredients

Nutritional value per serving:

Calories: **433 kcal**
Proteins: **25 grams**
Fats: **20 grams**
Carbohydrates: **35 grams**

Ingredients:

- Duck breast with skin: 2 pieces
- Oranges: 2 pieces
- Cranberries: 200 g
- Sugar: 2 tablespoons
- Cinnamon: ½ teaspoon
- Star anise: 1 piece
- Butter: 30 g
- Olive oil: 90 ml
- Thyme: 2 sprigs
- Honey: 1 tablespoon
- Wine vinegar: 15 ml
- Arugula: 65 g
- Pine nuts: 30 g
- Salt: to taste
- Ground black pepper: to taste

Cooking instructions:

1. Lightly score the skin on the duck breast, season with salt and pepper, and brush with olive oil. Heat 15 g of butter and 10 ml of olive oil over low heat in a skillet. Add the thyme to the pan, then place the duck breast skin-side down and cook for 4-5 minutes without flipping, until the skin is golden brown. Then, flip the duck breast and increase the heat, searing the meat on all sides for 2-3 min each.

2. In a saucepan, heat the cranberries with the juice of one orange, cinnamon, and star anise for five minutes. Then, strain the cranberries through a sieve. Add 50 ml of water to the resulting puree and return it to the heat. Season with salt and pepper, and add 15 g of butter. Stir for 30 seconds until a smooth consistency is achieved.

3. Peel the orange and cut out beautiful fillets, avoiding the white membranes. Do not discard the orange trimmings. Squeeze the juice from the orange trimmings, add honey, vinegar, salt, and pepper, and whisk. Then, while continuing to whisk, gradually pour in 50 ml of olive oil.

4. Slice the warm duck into thin slices, add 2-3 tablespoons of cranberry sauce, and mix. Mix the arugula with the orange dressing, place it on a serving plate, top with slices of duck, drizzle cranberry sauce over both the duck and the salad, arrange the orange segments on top, and sprinkle the finished salad with toasted pine nuts.

Salad with roasted pear, corn, and bulgur

◆ 4 servings

◆ 25 min

◆ 15 ingredients

Nutritional value per serving:

Calories: **779 kcal**

Proteins: **14 grams**

Fats: **51 grams**

Carbohydrates: **63 grams**

Ingredients:

- Conference pears: 2 pieces
- Bulgur: 100 g
- Apple cider vinegar: 40 ml
- Kimchi sauce: 2 tablespoons
- Thyme: 2 sprigs
- Rosemary: 1 sprig
- Refined olive oil: 20 ml
- Extra virgin olive oil: 60 ml

- Dijon mustard: 20 g
- Maple syrup: 20 ml
- Lemon juice: ½ teaspoon
- Corn salad: 80 g
- Blue cheese: 50 g
- Walnuts: to taste
- Salt: to taste

Cooking instructions:

1. Cook the bulgur until tender in salted water.

2. Cut one pear into large random slices. Cut the second one into slightly smaller pieces.

3. Mix apple cider vinegar, maple syrup, and kimchi, and marinate the small pieces of pear in this sauce.

4. Grill the pear slices in frying olive oil with sprigs of thyme and rosemary.

5. Mix extra virgin olive oil, mustard, maple syrup, salt, lemon juice, and a spoonful of the pear marinade. Dress cooked bulgur and corn in a separate bowl with this sauce.

6. On a plate, layer the bulgur, then add the marinated pear pieces, followed by the corn salad and the grilled pear slices. Sprinkle with pieces of blue cheese and grated walnuts. Drizzle with the mustard sauce and marinade.

Warm salad with chicken and spinach

- ◆ 4 servings
- ◆ 15 min
- ◆ 8 ingredients

Nutritional value per serving:

Calories: **439 kcal**
Proteins: **20 grams**
Fats: **28 grams**
Carbohydrates: **27 grams**

Ingredients:

- Spinach: 100 g
- Chicken fillet: 200 g
- White bread: 150 g
- Pine nuts: 100 g

- Garlic: 2 cloves
- Olive oil: 50 ml
- Salt: to taste
- Fresh pepper: to taste

Cooking instructions:

1. Heat a skillet with a small amount of olive oil. Cut the chicken fillet into large slices and fry them over high heat for five minutes until golden and crispy.

2. One minute before the chicken is done, add the spinach, sauté it briefly, mix, and remove the skillet from the heat. Season with salt and pepper to taste.

3. Remove the crust from the bread and crumble the inside by hand or chop it with a knife or blender. Sauté the bread crumbs in a skillet for five minutes with two tablespoons of olive oil, pine nuts, and finely chopped garlic. Remove the skillet from the heat when the crumbs dry out and the nuts become golden.

4. Transfer the chicken with spinach to a salad bowl, sprinkle with the mixture of bread crumbs, garlic, and nuts, and serve immediately.

Notes

Warm salad with fried cheese

◆ 4 servings
◆ 20 min
◆ 9 ingredients

Nutritional value per serving:
Calories: **439 kcal**
Proteins: **20 grams**
Fats: **28 grams**
Carbohydrates: **27 grams**

Ingredients:

• Tomatoes: 1 piece
• Camembert cheese: 120 g
• Mixed salad leaves: 1 bunch
• Cucumbers: ½ piece
• Wheat flour: 1 tablespoon

• Olive oil with Italian herbs: 4 tablespoons
• Pine nuts: 20 g
• Olive oil: 3 tablespoons
• Red onion: ⅓ head

Cooking instructions:

1. Cut the cheese into 1 cm thick slices and coat them in flour.

2. Place the slices on a preheated grill pan with 2 tablespoons of olive oil. Flip them over.

3. Sauté the pine nuts lightly in 1 tablespoon of oil.

4. Cut the tomatoes and cucumbers into large pieces. Slice the onion into half-rings.

5. Tear the salad leaves into large pieces and place them as the bottom layer, then add the vegetables, followed by the cheese and pine nuts.

Notes

Warm salad with chicken breast

◆ 4 servings
◆ 20 min
◆ 14 ingredients

Nutritional value per serving:
Calories: **689 kcal**
Proteins: **29 grams**
Fats: **63 grams**
Carbohydrates: **7 grams**

Ingredients:

- Olive oil: 150 ml
- Chicken breast: 1 piece
- Red onion: ½ head
- Romaine lettuce: 200 g
- Lemon: ½ piece

- Avocado: 1 piece
- Dried tomatoes: 3 pieces
- Basil leaves: 6 pieces
- Almonds: 40 g
- Mozzarella cheese: 150 g

- Salt: to taste
- Ground black pepper: to taste
- Balsamic vinegar: 1 tablespoon
- Bacon: 50 g

Cooking instructions:

1. Line a larger baking tray with parchment paper, place the bacon on it, cover with a second piece of parchment, and press down with another baking tray on top. Place in a preheated oven at 400 degrees for 10–15 minutes. The result should be firm, flat bacon strips.

2. Finely chop the onion. Wash the romaine lettuce leaves and chop them roughly. Remove the tomatoes from the jar, let the oil drain, and cut each wedge into five pieces.

3. Peel the avocado, remove the pit, cut it in half, and then slice each half into thin wedges. Drizzle the avocado with lemon juice. Toast the almonds in the oven until golden brown. Make the dressing by mixing 100 ml of olive oil with balsamic vinegar.

4. Cut the chicken breast into pieces so that each fillet yields 12 pieces. Heat olive oil in a skillet and fry the chicken in it. This will take about five minutes.

5. Add the finely chopped onion to the chicken and, stirring, cook until caramelized. Then add the salad, almonds, tomatoes, mozzarella, and basil leaves to the skillet. Check for salt and pepper.

6. Add the avocado and serve immediately, drizzled with the dressing.

Warm green bean salad

◆ 4 servings
◆ 15 min
◆ 7 ingredients

Nutritional value per serving:
Calories: **297 kcal**
Proteins: **7 grams**
Fats: **24 grams**
Carbohydrates: **17 grams**

Ingredients:

• Cherry tomatoes: 400 g

• Green beans: 800 g

• Olive oil: 4 tablespoons

• Lemon: 2 pieces

• Fresh basil: 10 stems

• Sea salt: to taste

• Ground black pepper: to taste

Cooking instructions:

1. Steam the green beans or boil them in boiling water for 2-3 minutes.

2. While the green beans are cooking, cut each tomato in half.

3. Squeeze the juice from the lemons, mix it with the olive oil, add salt, pepper, basil, and sesame seeds.

4. Dress the halved cherry tomatoes with the prepared sauce.

5. Add the hot green beans to the bowl with the tomatoes in the sauce. Toss and serve.

Notes

Tuna salad

◆ 4 servings
◆ 35 min
◆ 6 ingredients

Nutritional value per serving:

Calories: **143 kcal**
Proteins: **16 grams**
Fats: **7 grams**
Carbohydrates: **4 grams**

Ingredients:

• Canned tuna in its juice: 1 can
• Chicken eggs: 4 pieces
• Onion: 1 piece
• Lemon juice: 15 ml
• Fresh herbs: to taste
• Balsamic vinegar: to taste

Cooking instructions:

1. Dice the onion and eggs, drain the juice from the tuna, and add it to the other ingredients.

2. Finely chop the herbs. Squeeze the juice from half a lemon. Drizzle with vinegar, and season with salt and pepper.

Notes

Diet salad with shrimp and avocado

◆ 4 servings
◆ 10 min
◆ 7 ingredients

Nutritional value per serving:

Calories: **559 kcal**
Proteins: **28 grams**
Fats: **44 grams**
Carbohydrates: **11 grams**

Ingredients:

- Avocado: 4 pieces
- Shrimp: 400 g
- Cucumbers: 4 pieces
- Cheese: 80 g
- Garlic: 4 cloves
- Lemon: 4 pieces
- Olive oil: 4 tablespoons

Cooking instructions:

1. Boil the shrimp for 1.5–2 minutes, then peel them.

2. Cut the avocado into cubes.

3. Slice the cucumbers.

4. Place everything in one bowl.

5. Prepare the dressing: grate the garlic, pour in the olive oil, and squeeze the juice from half a lemon.

Notes

Meat salad with vegetables

◆ 4 servings
◆ 60 min
◆ 10 ingredients

Nutritional value per serving:

Calories: **351 kcal**
Proteins: **26 grams**
Fats: **21 grams**
Carbohydrates: **18 grams**

Ingredients:

• Sweet peppers: 4 pieces
• Lean beef: 800 g
• Tomatoes: 6 pieces
• Carrots: 2 pieces
• Onion: 4 pieces

• Gherkins: 200 g
• Garlic: 2 cloves
• Parsley: 1 bunch
• Lemon: 1 piece
• Olive oil: 100 ml

Cooking instructions:

1. Cut the meat into pieces (approximately 1.5x10 cm), and cook it in a skillet until done, seasoning with salt to taste. Five minutes before it's done, squeeze half a lemon over the meat and add the chopped garlic.

2. Grate the carrots on a coarse grater, drizzle with the juice of half a lemon, and set aside to marinate.

3. Cut the peppers into wedges (it's best to use peppers of different colors), and sauté them lightly for about 3 minutes. Add them to the meat. Cut the tomatoes into quarters and lightly sauté them in the skillet for 2-3 minutes. Add them to the meat with the peppers. Cut the onion into quarters and lightly sauté it in the skillet for 4 minutes. Add it to the main dish.

4. Slice the gherkins crosswise. Add them to the salad. Then add the carrots along with the juice and the finely chopped parsley.

5.Pour the prepared dressing over the shrimp, avocado, and cucumbers in the bowl. Gently mix all the ingredients to ensure they are evenly coated with the dressing. Optionally, sprinkle the salad with a pinch of salt, freshly ground black pepper, and garnish with fresh herbs such as cilantro or parsley.

6. Serve immediately as a light and healthy dish.

Meat salad with nuts

- ◆ 4 servings
- ◆ 30 min
- ◆ 6 ingredients

Nutritional value per serving:

Calories: **830 kcal**

Proteins: **57 grams**

Fats: **64 grams**

Carbohydrates: **10 grams**

Ingredients:

- Beef: 1 kg
- Walnuts: 200 g
- Ground black pepper: to taste
- Tomatoes: 2 pieces
- Cucumbers: 2 pieces
- Basil: 100 g
- Sour cream: 2 tablespoons
- Mustard: 2 teaspoons
- Salt: to taste

Cooking instructions:

1. Boil the meat in salted water, cool it down, and cut it into strips or cubes.

2. Cut the cucumbers and tomatoes into pieces of your choice.

3. Crush the nuts in a mortar or pass them through a meat grinder.

4. Combine all the ingredients, season with salt and pepper, and dress with sour cream and mustard to taste, mixing well.

Notes

Keto salad with veal liver

◆ 4 servings
◆ 10 min
◆ 10 ingredients

Nutritional value per serving:
Calories: **558 kcal**
Proteins: **25 grams**
Fats: **41 grams**
Carbohydrates: **19 grams**

Ingredients:

• Napa cabbage: 200 g
• Veal liver: 400 g
• Arugula: 40 g
• Spinach: 20 g
• Dill: 1 bunch

• Avocado: 2 pieces
• Sun-dried tomatoes: 10 pieces
• Refined olive oil: 4 tablespoons
• Extra virgin olive oil: 2 tablespoons
• Sea salt: to taste

Cooking instructions:

1. Finely chop the Napa cabbage.

2. Combine with coarsely chopped arugula.

3. Add the spinach and mix well.

4. Finely chop the avocado, season with salt, and drizzle with apple cider vinegar.

5. Add to the salad and dress with unrefined oil.

6. Cut the liver into long thin strips. Place it in a heated skillet with refined oil. After 2–3 minutes, season with salt and stir. Sauté for another 3 minutes.

7. Finely chop the dill and sun-dried tomatoes.

8. Combine all the ingredients, mix well, season with salt, and serve.

Notes

Notes

Dinner

Vegetable risotto with onion and carrots

- ◆ 4 servings
- ◆ 25 min
- ◆ 8 ingredients

Nutritional value per serving:

Calories: **385 kcal**
Proteins: **6 grams**
Fats: **16 grams**
Carbohydrates: **56 grams**

Ingredients:

- Basmati rice: 200 g
- Onion: 1 head
- Carrot: 1 piece
- Sweet pepper: 200 g
- Olive oil: 3 tablespoons
- Canned corn: 150 g
- Salt: to taste
- Greens: to taste

Cooking instructions:

1. Rinse the rice in cold water until the water runs clear. Place it in a pot, cover with it cold water, and set it on the heat. Bring to a boil, season with salt (to taste), then reduce the heat. Cook on low heat for 12 minutes.

2. Slice the onion into half-rings and dice the carrot into small cubes. Sauté them in a skillet with olive oil.

3. Remove the seeds from the pepper, rinse it, and cut it into cubes.

4. Add the rice, canned corn, and pepper to the skillet with the onion and carrot, and mix everything thoroughly.

5. When serving, garnish with herbs.

Notes

Pumpkin risotto

◆ 4 servings
◆ 30 min
◆ 9 ingredients

Nutritional value per serving:

Calories: **709 kcal**
Proteins: **16 grams**
Fats: **43 grams**
Carbohydrates: **104 grams**

Ingredients:

• Basmati rice: 700 g

• Pumpkin: 700 g

• Shallots: 4 heads

• Butter: 150 g

• Chicken broth: 1½ L

• Brandy: 100 ml

• Chopped parsley: 6 tablespoons

• Garlic: 6 cloves

• Grated Parmesan cheese: to taste

Cooking instructions:

1. Melt the butter and sauté the finely chopped shallots in a deep skillet. Add the minced garlic and cook for another minute. Once the shallots soften slightly, add the diced pumpkin, mix it with the shallots, and fry for 10 minutes over high heat, stirring constantly.

2. After 10 minutes, pour the brandy into the pan, mix it with the roasted pumpkin, reduce the heat, and let it simmer, stirring occasionally with a spatula to prevent the contents from burning.

3. When the pumpkin softens enough that the shape of the cubes can be easily broken with a light press of a spoon, take a wooden masher and mash the pumpkin directly in the pan until it turns into an orange purée. Then, add the rice to this purée, mix it with the pumpkin, and fry for about 2 minutes.

4. Now, pour the chicken broth into the pan and let it cook for 12 minutes, occasionally returning to stir the risotto. If the liquid evaporates too quickly, add more broth. After 12 minutes, with the rice and pumpkin. Cover the pan with a lid and turn off the heat. After another 2 minutes, the risotto can be served, topped with grated Parmesan.

Notes

Cocotte with red fish

- ◆ 4 servings
- ◆ 20 min
- ◆ 8 ingredients

Nutritional value per serving:

Calories: **260 kcal**

Proteins: **27 grams**

Fats: **14 grams**

Carbohydrates: **3 grams**

Ingredients:

- Redfish: 500 g
- Cream cheese: 130 g
- Garlic: 2 cloves
- Cucumbers: 2 pieces

- Parsley: to taste
- Provençal herbs: to taste
- Freshly ground black pepper: to taste
- Smoked paprika: to taste

Cooking instructions:

1. Marinate any redfish with spices of your choice, such as Provençal herbs or smoked paprika. Brush with olive oil on both sides. Bake the fish in the oven for 10 minutes at 400 degrees Fahrenheit. Remove the skin, remove the bones, and flake it with a fork.

2. Mix the cream cheese with the garlic (pressed) and sprinkle in some freshly ground black pepper. Add this mixture to the fish and stir to combine.

3. Using a vegetable peeler, slice the cucumber into thin strips. Place the fish on bread or focaccia, top it with the cucumber, and serve. If desired, sprinkle with finely chopped parsley.

Notes

Red beans with tuna and noodles

◆ 4 servings
◆ 20 min
◆ 11 ingredients

Nutritional value per serving:

Calories: **332 kcal**
Proteins: **18 grams**
Fats: **11 grams**
Carbohydrates: **39 grams**

Ingredients:

- Red beans: 267 g
- Canned tuna in its own juice: 67 g
- Red onion: 0.5 piece
- Arugula: 100 g
- Olive oil: 35 ml
- Garlic: 3 cloves
- Lemon: ¾ piece
- Chicken broth: 0.7 L
- Egg noodles: 170g
- Salt: to taste
- Ground black pepper: to taste

Cooking instructions:

1. Combine the cooked beans (canned is fine) with finely chopped red onion, arugula, crushed garlic, olive oil, lemon juice, and the tuna fillet torn into small pieces.

2. Cook the egg noodles until they are hyper-al dense. If the package says to boil the noodles for ten minutes, cook them for eight; if it says twelve minutes, cook them for ten. Drain the water.

3. In a deep skillet, heat the chicken broth, then add the noodles and the beans with tuna. Stir and let simmer on low heat for another two minutes. Serve immediately.

Notes

Pikeperch with white wine sauce

◆ 4 servings
◆ 45 min
◆ 13 ingredients

Nutritional value per serving:

Calories: **769 kcal**
Proteins: **19 grams**
Fats: **66 grams**
Carbohydrates: **17 grams**

Ingredients:

- Pikeperch fillet: 1 piece
- Cauliflower: 500 g
- Butter: 200 g
- Truffle oil: 15 ml:
- Cream: 100 ml:
- Thyme: 6 sprigs
- Garlic: 7 cloves
- 33% cream: 250 ml
- Chicken broth: 400 ml
- Dry white wine: 200 ml
- Spinach: 70 g
- Salt: to taste
- Ground black pepper: to taste

Cooking instructions:

1. Break the cauliflower into small florets. Place the cauliflower in a pot with water and boil for 10–15 minutes after it starts boiling. The cauliflower should not turn mush but break easily into smaller florets with a fork.

2. Transfer the cauliflower to a blender and blend until smooth. Add 30 g of butter, truffle oil, and 100 ml of cream to the blender and blend until smooth. Season the purée with salt to taste.

3. Crush 3 garlic cloves and lightly sauté them with 3 thyme sprigs in a dry skillet. Once the aroma is released, pour in the wine and let it reduce slightly to remove the alcohol smell. Once the smell of alcohol has dissipated, add the butter and chicken broth to the skillet. When the butter has melted and the broth begins to boil, add 150 ml of cream. Reduce the sauce over low heat, stirring, until it reaches the consistency of liquid sour cream. Remove the garlic and thyme from the sauce and pour it into a bowl.

4. Prepare the spinach. Crush 2 more garlic cloves and place them in a heated, clean skillet. Pour a little vegetable oil into the skillet, add the spinach, and include a piece of butter. Sauté the spinach quickly, stirring constantly. Once it becomes slightly softer and wilts, season with salt. Stir, remove the skillet from the heat, and transfer the spinach to a plate.

5. Prepare the pikeperch. Cut the fillet crosswise into pieces about 2–3 cm thick. Heat a skillet with a small amount of vegetable oil. Fry the pieces of pikeperch on both sides until golden brown, approximately 2–3 minutes per side, depending on the thickness. Make sure the fish is cooked through but not overdone.

6. For serving: place the cauliflower purée on a plate, add the spinach next to it, and top with the fried pieces of pikeperch. Drizzle the dish with the prepared creamy sauce. Optionally, garnish with fresh herbs such as thyme or parsley. Serve immediately while the dish is hot.

Cod with vegetable topping

- ◆ 4 servings
- ◆ 15 min
- ◆ 8 ingredients

Nutritional value per serving:
Calories: **242 kcal**
Proteins: **24 grams**
Fats: **16 grams**
Carbohydrates: **1 grams**

Ingredients:

- Cod fillet: 500 g
- Olive oil: 1 tablespoons
- Coarse sea salt: a pinch
- Marinated chili pepper: 20 g

- Canned jalapeño pepper: 20 g
- Mayonnaise: 2 tablespoons
- Ground black pepper: to taste
- Pink Himalayan salt: to taste

Cooking instructions:

1. Chop the jalapeño peppers. Do the same with the chili pepper.

2. Heat the olive oil with a pinch of coarse sea salt in a skillet. Place the cod fillet in the skillet. After 2 minutes, flip the cod fillet and reduce the heat. Season with Himalayan salt and cover with a splatter guard lid. After 3–4 minutes, flip the cod fillet again. Reduce the heat to minimum.

3. After 2–3 minutes, transfer to a plate and spread with mayonnaise. Season with black pepper. Top with the vegetable topping and serve.

Meat french style

◆ 4 servings
◆ 120 min
◆ 9 ingredients

Nutritional value per serving:

Calories: **506 kcal**
Proteins: **29 grams**
Fats: **34 grams**
Carbohydrates: **21 grams**

Ingredients:

• Pork: 700 g
• Tomatoes: 3 pieces
• Cheese: 300 g
• Mayonnaise: 200 g
• Potatoes: 5 pieces

• Onions: 2 heads
• Herbs spice mix: to taste
• Salt: to taste
• Ground black pepper: to taste

Cooking instructions:

1. Cut the meat into thin steaks. Tenderize well on each side. Slice the onion into half rings.

2. Peel the potatoes and slice them into thin rounds.

3. Line a baking sheet with foil, lightly greasing it with sunflower oil. Place the onion as the first layer, followed by the potatoes on top. Season with salt to taste.

4. Place the meat on top of the potatoes. Season with herbs, salt, and pepper to taste.

5. Slice the tomatoes into thin rounds. Place the tomatoes on the meat, distributing 1–2 slices on each steak.

6. Grate the cheese on a coarse grater. Pour the mayonnaise into a deep bowl. Add the cheese and stir until smooth.

7. Spread the cheese mixture on top of each piece. Cover with foil and place in the oven for 40 min. The temperature should be 400 degrees.

Notes

Roast beef sous vide

- ◆ 4 servings
- ◆ 300 min
- ◆ 6 ingredients

Nutritional value per serving:

Calories: **371 kcal**
Proteins: **28 grams**
Fats: **39 grams**
Carbohydrates: **0 grams**

Ingredients:

- Beef: 600 g
- Sea Salt: 56 g
- Ground Black Pepper: to taste
- Vegetable oil: 10 ml
- Butter: 16 g
- Salt: to taste

Cooking instructions:

1. Prepare all the ingredients. Bring the water to a boil. Trim the beef tenderloin of any membranes.

2. Dissolve the salt in 2 liters of cold water and soak the tenderloin in it for 2 hours.

3. Rinse the meat under running water, pat it dry, and rub it with ground black pepper and a small amount of vegetable oil. Place the tenderloin in a bag and vacuum seal it.

4. Put the meat in boiling water to cook for 3-4 hours.

5. After cooking, remove the tenderloin from the bag and pat it dry with a paper towel.

6. In a large skillet, heat the butter. Sear the tenderloin on all sides until golden brown.

7. The translation is: "Let the finished roast beef rest for 5–10 minutes before slicing.

8. Serve the roast beef, slicing it into thin pieces.

Notes

Braised beef

◆ 4 servings
◆ 100 min
◆ 10 ingredients

Nutritional value per serving:

Calories: **349 kcal**
Proteins: **30 grams**
Fats: **27 grams**
Carbohydrates: **10 grams**

Ingredients:

• Beef: 600 g

• Onion: 200 g

• Carrot: 200 g

• Allspice (whole berries): 5 pieces

• Bay leaves: 3 pieces

• Paprika: 1 teaspoon

• Ground chili pepper: to taste

• Salt: to taste

• Ground black pepper: to taste

• Vegetable oil: 30 ml

Cooking instructions:

1. Remove any membranes and ligaments from the beef, and cut it into pieces (as desired).

2. Heat the oil in a deep skillet and sauté the beef. Then pour a cup of boiling water over the meat. Add the allspice and bay leaves, bring to a boil. Simmer on low heat with the lid on for about 40 min.

3. Peel the onion, cut it into large half-rings, and then cut the half-rings in half again.

4. Peel the carrot and cut it into wedges. Add the onion and carrot to the meat. Mix well.

5. Add salt and spices. Then continue to simmer the beef on low heat with the lid on for another hour.

Notes

Turkey fillet braised with sour cream

- ◆ 4 servings
- ◆ 35 min
- ◆ 6 ingredients

Nutritional value per serving:
Calories: **353 kcal**
Proteins: **50 grams**
Fats: **3 grams**
Carbohydrates: **6 grams**

Ingredients:

- Turkey fillet: 1 kg
- Sour cream (10% fat): 2 tablespoons
- Soy sauce: 2 tablespoons
- Onion: 1 piece
- Garlic: 3 cloves
- Pepper blend: to taste

Cooking instructions:

1. Cut the turkey fillet, place it in a skillet, and braise over medium heat for 10–15 minutes.

2. Chop the onion, add it to the fillet, and continue braising for about 5 min until the onion softens.

3. Mince the garlic and add it to the skillet with the turkey.

4. Next, add the sour cream, soy sauce, pepper blend, and salt to taste. Mix everything well, add a little boiled water to make the sauce more liquid, and simmer for another 10 minutes until it thickens.

Notes

Turkey baked with potatoes

- ◆ 4 servings
- ◆ 75 min
- ◆ 10 ingredients

Nutritional value per serving:

Calories: **434 kcal**
Proteins: **20 grams**
Fats: **23 grams**
Carbohydrates: **39 grams**

Ingredients:

- Turkey drumsticks: 2 pieces
- Potatoes: 4 pieces
- Olive oil: 50 ml
- Red onion: ½ bulb
- Garlic: 3 cloves

- Dried basil: to taste
- Rosemary: to taste
- Ground black pepper: to taste
- Sea salt: to taste
- Prunes: 8 pieces

Cooking instructions:

1. Drizzle the turkey drumsticks with olive oil, and sprinkle with salt, pepper, rosemary, and basil. Add the chopped onion and the garlic cloves cut into quarters. Rub the turkey pieces well with the mixture.

2. Place the meat on aluminum foil and top with prunes.

3. Peel the potatoes and slice them into medium-thick rounds. Drizzle with oil, season with salt and pepper, and sprinkle with rosemary. Arrange the potatoes around the turkey.

4. Cover the meat and potatoes with foil, tucking in the edges. Place in a preheated oven at 200 degrees Celsius (about 392 degrees. Fahrenheit) for 45 minutes.

5. Remove the parcel from the oven, cut the foil, and return it to the oven to brown for 10 minutes at 400 degrees Fahrenheit (about 200 degrees.

Notes

Roast turkey

- ◆ 4 servings
- ◆ 210 min
- ◆ 17 ingredients

Nutritional value per serving:

Calories: **980 kcal**
Proteins: **153 grams**
Fats: **20 grams**
Carbohydrates: **45 grams**

Ingredients:

- Turkey: 2.7 kg
- Salt: 333 g
- Honey: 167 g
- Lemon: 2¾ pieces
- Bay leaves: 1¼ pieces
- Garlic: 1¾ heads
- Salt: to taste
- Ground black pepper: to taste
- Black peppercorns: 1¼ teaspoons
- Parsley: 1 bunch
- Thyme: 1 bunch
- Clarified butter: 20 ml
- Ground turkey: 300 g
- Egg white: 1¼ pieces
- 33% cream: 33 ml
- Rosemary: 7 g
- Turkey broth: 1⁄₁₀ liters

Cooking instructions:

1. Clean the turkey, separate the drumsticks and thighs, and remove the bones from the thighs, leaving the skin intact. Remove the backbone from the breast and detach the wings.

2. Mix the coarse salt, honey, peppercorns, halved lemons, two halved heads of garlic, a bunch of parsley, and a bunch of thyme in a large pot. Fill with water and bring to a boil, then remove from heat and let cool. Submerge the drumsticks and breast in the broth for 3 hours.

3. Preheat the oven to 428 degrees. Remove the turkey from the marinade and pat it dry with paper towels. Brush with clarified butter, and season with salt and pepper.

4. In a large pot, mix the coarse salt, honey, peppercorns, halved lemons, two halved heads of garlic, a bunch of parsley, and a bunch of thyme. Fill with water and bring to a boil, then remove from heat and let cool. Submerge the drumsticks and breast in the broth for 3 hours.

5. Submerge the rolls in a wide saucepan with gently simmering water and cook for 35–45 minutes. Then remove them and unwrap the plastic. Place them on a baking sheet with the drumsticks and bake for 2 hours in the oven at 356 degrees Fahrenheit until golden brown.

French-style salmon steaks

- ◆ 4 servings
- ◆ 30 min
- ◆ 12 ingredients

Nutritional value per serving:

Calories: **388 kcal**

Proteins: **42 grams**

Fats: **18 grams**

Carbohydrates: **12 grams**

Ingredients:

- Salmon steaks: 4 pieces
- Shallots: 3 heads
- Green onions: 1 bunch
- Tarragon: 1 bunch
- Parsley: 1 bunch
- Basil: 1 bunch
- Lemon: 1 piece
- Balsamic vinegar: 20 ml
- Olive oil: 10 ml
- Flaxseed oil: 10 ml
- Salt: ½ teaspoon
- Tomatoes: 400 g

Cooking instructions:

1. Preheat the oven to 302 °F.

2. Lightly salt the fish, drizzle with olive oil, wrap it in foil, and bake in the preheated oven for 10 min.

3. Then open the foil and place the fish under the hot grill for 10 minutes, until golden brown.

4. Peel and chop the shallots. Finely chop the herbs.

5. Peel the tomatoes, remove the seeds and juice, and finely chop the flesh. The juice can be used to dress other dishes.

6. Combine the chopped tomatoes with the shallots and herbs, then add the lemon juice, balsamic vinegar, and flaxseed oil. Mix everything well.

7. Pat the cooked fish with a paper towel to remove excess oil, and serve with the tomato salad.

Notes

Eggplant steaks

- ◆ 4 servings
- ◆ 30 min
- ◆ 10 ingredients

Nutritional value per serving:

Calories: **366 kcal**
Proteins: **13 grams**
Fats: **30 grams**
Carbohydrates: **9 grams**

Ingredients:

- Eggplant: 1 piece
- Tomatoes: 2 pieces
- Arugula: 150 g
- Vegetable oil: to taste
- Parmesan cheese: 150 g

- Olive oil: 4 tablespoons
- Garlic: 1 clove
- White wine vinegar: 1 tablespoon
- Greek olives: 6 pieces
- Basil leaves: 2 tablespoons

Cooking instructions:

1. Preheat the grill. Slice the eggplant into 4 thin pieces and brush with oil. Place on the grill, sprinkle with salt, and grill for 10 minutes until golden brown, turning once.

2. Place the tomato quarters on the grill, lightly brush with oil, and sprinkle with salt. Cook for 2 minutes, then transfer to a plate with the eggplants. Let cool.

3. On 4 serving plates, arrange the arugula leaves, then the eggplant, and top with the tomatoes and pieces of Parmesan.

4. Whisk together the oil, vinegar, and minced garlic in a small bowl. Add the finely chopped olives and salt. Drizzle the sauce over the eggplants. Serve warm.

Notes

Steaks with sautéed shallots

- ◆ 4 servings
- ◆ 40 min
- ◆ 7 ingredients

Nutritional value per serving:
Calories: **337 kcal**
Proteins: **46 grams**
Fats: **48 grams**
Carbohydrates: **6 grams**

Ingredients:

- Olive oil: 2 tablespoons
- Shallots: 2 pieces
- Garlic: 2 cloves
- Beef steak: 4 pieces

- Vegetable oil: 4 tablespoons
- Salt: to taste
- Freshly ground black pepper: to taste

Cooking instructions:

1. Preheat the oven to 788°F. Grease a baking dish with olive oil (1 tablespoon). Place the shallots and garlic in the dish. Cover with aluminum foil. Bake in the oven until the shallots are soft and the garlic is golden (about 30 minutes).

2. Cool the shallots and garlic, then chop everything finely.

3. Heat a large skillet over medium heat. Brush the beef fillets with Worcestershire sauce on both sides, then season with salt and pepper. Pour 2 tablespoons of vegetable oil with additives into the skillet.

4. Place the fillets in the skillet and cook until a crust forms (about 3 minutes). Flip and cook for another 4 minutes.

5. Transfer the skillet to the oven and cook for an additional 4-5 minutes.

6. Transfer the fillets to a plate. Add the chopped shallots and garlic. Cook for 1-2 minutes.

7. Place a spoonful of the shallot and garlic mixture on each steak.

Notes

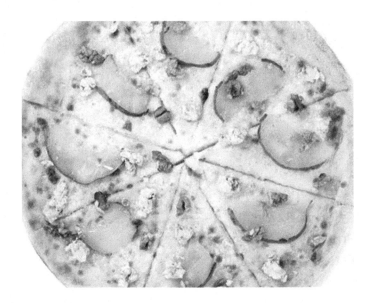

Pizza with blue cheese and pear

- ◆ 4 servings
- ◆ 30 min
- ◆ 8 ingredients

Nutritional value per serving:

Calories: **295 kcal**
Proteins: **12 grams**
Fats: **10 grams**
Carbohydrates: **41 grams**

Ingredients:

- Wheat flour: 200 g
- Water: 100 ml
- Salt: 3 g
- Olive oil: 2 ml

- Dry yeast
- Gorgonzola cheese: 67 g
- Mozzarella cheese: 80 g
- Pears: ¾ piece

Cooking instructions:

1. Combine the flour, water, olive oil, salt, and yeast for the dough. Knead the dough and let it rest in a warm place for 30 minutes. You will need 150 g of dough for one pizza.

2. Roll it out with a rolling pin on a floured surface into a circle 1.5 mm thick. Then, spread 120 g of pre-grated mozzarella and small pieces of Gorgonzola on the rolled-out dough. The key is not to buy fresh mozzarella for this purpose, as it cannot be grated, so you should choose a firmer mozzarella suitable for pizza.

3. It is necessary to place the pizza in the oven preheated to 360 degrees for seven to ten minutes. You should stay vigilant and check the pizza for doneness. The dough should be golden brown but not burnt, and the cheese should melt without turning into a crust.

4. You can take it out as soon as the pizza appears to be ready. With a tablespoon, spread the melted pieces of Gorgonzola so that the entire pizza surface is covered with a thin layer of cheese. You can leave the crust without cheese or you can choose to cover it — it's up to you.

Notes

Carbonara pasta with zucchini

- ◆ 4 servings
- ◆ 15 min
- ◆ 9 ingredients

Nutritional value per serving:

Calories: **827 kcal**

Proteins: **36 grams**

Fats: **51 grams**

Carbohydrates: **55 grams**

Ingredients:

- Zucchini: 1½ pieces
- Bacon: 320 g
- Olive oil: 16 ml
- Penne pasta: 240 g
- Chicken eggs: 2½ pieces
- Wheat flour: 40 g
- Grated Parmesan cheese: 40 g
- Sea salt: to taste
- Cream: 120 ml

Cooking instructions:

1. In a deep skillet, heat olive oil and sauté the bacon (it's easiest to cut it into cubes).

2. Cut the zucchini into your preferred shapes and add them to the bacon. Sauté for another 7 min.

3. Add the pasta to boiling water and cook until al dente.

4. The most challenging part of this pasta is the sauce. So, add only the yolks—one yolk per serving (this recipe is for three servings). For each yolk, add 30 ml of milk or cream and a little flour, then mix everything together.

5. When the zucchini are ready, add the cooked pasta to them, remove from heat, and listen. Aggressive sizzling is unsuitable for our sauce, so we wait for it to stop before adding it. Mix everything and add a little pasta water if needed.

6. When serving, garnish with herbs and grated Parmesan.

Notes

Vegetable satay

- ◆ 4 servings
- ◆ 15 min
- ◆ 8 ingredients

Nutritional value per serving:
Calories: **455 kcal**
Proteins: **5 grams**
Fats: **37 grams**
Carbohydrates: **28 grams**

Ingredients:

- Onion: 530 g
- Sweet bell pepper: 4 pieces
- Carrot: 2 pieces
- Olive oil: 4 tablespoons

- Butter: 4 pieces
- Mixed ground pepper: 2 teaspoons
- Salt: to taste
- Coarse sea salt: a pinch

Cooking instructions:

1. Chop the onion, carrot, and bell pepper into small pieces.

2. Heat the butter and olive oil in a pan.

3. Add 2 pinches of coarse salt. Place the vegetables into the oil. Add a mixture of peppers.

4. After 3–4 minutes, stir and reduce the heat to medium.

5. Cover with a lid and simmer for about 7–8 minutes, stirring occasionally.

6. Then add salt and stir.

7. After 1 minute, remove from heat and transfer to a plate.

Notes

Notes

Smoothie

Watermelon smoothie

♦ 2 servings
♦ 5 min
♦ 6 ingredients

Nutritional value per serving:
Calories: **314 kcal**
Proteins: **6 grams**
Fats: **2 grams**
Carbohydrates: **72 grams**

Ingredients:

• Raspberries: 7 pieces
• Strawberries: 7 pieces
• Banana: 1 piece

• Watermelon: 6 pieces
• Fruit juice: 250 ml
• Oatmeal: 2 tablespoons

Cooking instructions:

1. Peel the banana.

2. Cut everything into pieces and place in a blender.

3. Pour in the juice and blend.

Notes

Blueberry smoothie

- ◆ 2 servings
- ◆ 5 min
- ◆ 3 ingredients

Nutritional value per serving:

Calories: **205 kcal**

Proteins: **8 grams**

Fats: **9 grams**

Carbohydrates: **25 grams**

Ingredients:

- Blueberries: 60 g
- Milk: 500 ml

- Sugar: 2 teaspoons

Cooking instructions:

1. Blend the blueberries with the milk in a blender for 3 minutes.

2. Add sugar or honey and blend again.

Notes

Citrus smoothie with carrot

◆ 2 servings
◆ 10 min
◆ 4 ingredients

Nutritional value per serving:

Calories: **270 kcal**
Proteins: **6 grams**
Fats: **2 grams**
Carbohydrates: **59 grams**

Ingredients:

• Oranges: 2 pieces
• Apples: 2 pieces

• Carrots: 2 pieces
• Freshly squeezed orange juice: 400 ml

Cooking instructions:

1. Peel all the fruits and carrots. Blend all the ingredients in a blender until smooth.

2. Garnish with a slice of orange and mint.

Notes

Berry and banana smoothie

- ◆ 2 servings
- ◆ 5 min
- ◆ 5 ingredients

Nutritional value per serving:

Calories: **207 kcal**
Proteins: **6 grams**
Fats: **3 grams**
Carbohydrates: **40 grams**

Ingredients:

- Raspberries: 8¾ pieces
- Natural yogurt: ¾ cup
- Cherries: 8¾ pieces

- Strawberries: 8¾ pieces
- Bananas: 1¼ pieces

Cooking instructions:

1. Peel the bananas and cut them into pieces.

2. Blend the bananas and berries in a blender. Pour in the yogurt.

3. Blend until smooth.

Notes

Celery and orange smoothie

◆ 2 servings
◆ 15 min
◆ 3 ingredients

Nutritional value per serving:

Calories: **96 kcal**
Proteins: **4 grams**
Fats: **1 grams**
Carbohydrates: **20 grams**

Ingredients:

• Celery stalks: 4 pieces

• Oranges: 2 pieces

• Water: 2 cups

Cooking instructions:

1. Place the celery and orange slices into the blender cup.

2. After the first blending, add a cup of water.

3. Next, blend until frothy.

Notes

Emerald smoothie

- ◆ 2 servings
- ◆ 20 min
- ◆ 4 ingredients

Nutritional value per serving:

Calories: **331 kcal**

Proteins: **4 grams**

Fats: **1 grams**

Carbohydrates: **43 grams**

Ingredients:

- Pineapple: ½ piece
- Mandarins: 6 pieces
- Cilantro: 2 bunches
- Spinach: 50 g

Cooking instructions:

1. Blend all the ingredients in a blender until smooth.

2. Garnish with basil if desired.

Notes

Papaya and peach smoothie

- ◆ 2 servings
- ◆ 10 min
- ◆ 6 ingredients

Nutritional value per serving:

Calories: **94 kcal**

Proteins: **1 grams**

Fats: **0 grams**

Carbohydrates: **21 grams**

Ingredients:

- Papaya flesh: ½ cup
- Peach nectar: ½ cup
- Buttermilk: ¼ cup
- Sugar: 1¼ tablespoons
- Lime juice: 2 teaspoons
- Ice: 2½ pieces

Cooking instructions:

1. Combine the chopped papaya flesh, peach nectar, buttermilk, sugar, lime juice, and ice.

2. Blend until smooth. Serve immediately.

Notes

Apricot and kiwi smoothie

- ◆ 2 servings
- ◆ 5 min
- ◆ 4 ingredients

Nutritional value per serving:

Calories: **119 kcal**
Proteins: **2 grams**
Fats: **1 grams**
Carbohydrates: **28 grams**

Ingredients:

- Apricots: 5 pieces
- Kiwi: 2 pieces
- Cherries: 9 pieces
- Apple juice: 1 cup

Cooking instructions:

1. Peel the kiwi.

2. Cut the kiwi and apricots into pieces.

3. Place everything in the blender, pour in the juice, and blend.

Notes

Celery, carrot, and apple smoothie

- ◆ 2 servings
- ◆ 5 min
- ◆ 3 ingredients

Nutritional value per serving:

Calories: **414 kcal**
Proteins: **14 grams**
Fats: **4 grams**
Carbohydrates: **85 grams**

Ingredients:

- Carrot: 1 piece
- Apple: 1 piece
- Celery root: 3 pieces

Cooking instructions:

1. Peel the carrot and apple.

2. Cut everything into pieces and blend in a blender. Add water to taste.

Notes

Melon and strawberry smoothie

◆ 2 servings
◆ 10 min
◆ 4 ingredients

Nutritional value per serving:

Calories: **225 kcal**
Proteins: **6 grams**
Fats: **2 grams**
Carbohydrates: **45 grams**

Ingredients:

• Melon: 500 g
• Frozen strawberries: 2 cups

• Oatmeal: 2 tablespoons
• Vanilla milk: 6 tablespoons

Cooking instructions:

1. Place all the ingredients in the blender.

2. Blend until smooth.

Notes

Apple and celery stalk smoothie

◆ 2 servings
◆ 10 min
◆ 3 ingredients

Nutritional value per serving:

Calories: **106 kcal**
Proteins: **2 grams**
Fats: **1 grams**
Carbohydrates: **22 grams**

Ingredients:

• Apples: 2 pieces
• Celery stalks: 2 pieces

• Water: 2 cups

Cooking instructions:

1. Blend everything and serve.

Notes

Avocado, cucumber, and apple smoothie

◆ 2 servings
◆ 10 min
◆ 4 ingredients

Nutritional value per serving:

Calories: **284 kcal**
Proteins: **4 grams**
Fats: **17 grams**
Carbohydrates: **24 grams**

Ingredients:

• Avocados: 2 pieces
• Cucumbers: 2 pieces

• Apples: 2 pieces
• Water: 400 ml

Cooking instructions:

1. Peel the cucumber and avocado.

2. Slice the apple into wedges.

3. Add water.

4. Blend until smooth in a blender.

Notes

Celery and cucumber smoothie

◆ 2 servings
◆ 10 min
◆ 8 ingredients

Nutritional value per serving:

Calories: **60 kcal**
Proteins: **1 grams**
Fats: **5 grams**
Carbohydrates: **3 grams**

Ingredients:

• Celery: 90 g
• Cucumbers: 90 g
• Lemon juice: 2 tablespoons
• Extra virgin olive oil: 1 teaspoon

• Arugula: 30 g
• Sea salt: to taste
• Water: 200 ml
• Microgreens: to taste

Cooking instructions:

1. Peel the cucumber. Rinse the arugula.

2. Wash the celery.

3. Finely chop the cucumber, arugula, and celery.

4. Transfer the vegetables to the blender and add salt.

5. Add the olive oil.

6. Add the lemon juice and microgreens.

7. Add water to the blender. Blend until smooth.

Notes

Avocado and fresh raspberry smoothie

- ◆ 2 servings
- ◆ 10 min
- ◆ 4 ingredients

Nutritional value per serving:

Calories: **105 kcal**
Proteins: **1 grams**
Fats: **4 grams**
Carbohydrates: **15 grams**

Ingredients:

- Avocado: ½ piece
- Orange juice: ½ cup
- Raspberry juice: ½ cup
- Raspberries: 45 g

Cooking instructions:

1. Peel the avocado and place it in the blender.

2. Add orange juice, raspberry, and berries. Whisk until smooth and serve.

Notes

Broccoli, spinach, and fruit smoothie

◆ 2 servings
◆ 15 min
◆ 6 ingredients

Nutritional value per serving:

Calories: **96 kcal**
Proteins: **3 grams**
Fats: **1 grams**
Carbohydrates: **20 grams**

Ingredients:

• Carrot: 1 piece
• Broccoli florets
• Apple: 1 piece

• Oranges: 2 pieces
• Spinach: 75 g
• Orange juice: 250 ml

Cooking instructions:

1. Mix the chopped carrot and broccoli, then pour in the orange juice. Add the other vegetables and blend everything in a blender.

2. You can add some sunflower seeds.

Notes

Detox beet and avocado smoothie

◆ 2 servings
◆ 15 min
◆ 6 ingredients

Nutritional value per serving:
Calories: **315 kcal**
Proteins: **7 grams**
Fats: **10 grams**
Carbohydrates: **48 grams**

Ingredients:

- Beetroot: 2 pieces
- Avocados: 2 pieces
- Celery stalk: 1 piece
- Strawberries: 200 g
- Apples: 2 pieces
- Lemon juice: to taste

Cooking instructions:

1. Use a small beetroot.

2. Blend all the ingredients in a blender.

Notes

Zucchini smoothie

◆ 2 servings
◆ 15 min
◆ 7 ingredients

Nutritional value per serving:
Calories: **155 kcal**
Proteins: **8 grams**
Fats: **6 grams**
Carbohydrates: **35 grams**

Ingredients:

• Almond milk: 2 tablespoons
• Zucchini: 2 pieces
• Almond paste: 100 g
• Honey: 2 tablespoons
• Dates: 4 pieces
• Cinnamon: 1 teaspoon
• Ginger: 200 g

Cooking instructions:

1. Blend everything until smooth.

2. Garnish with cocoa nibs, dates, and goji berries.

Notes

Kefir vegetable smoothie

◆ 2 servings
◆ 15 min
◆ 7 ingredients

Nutritional value per serving:
Calories: **188 kcal**
Proteins: **16 grams**
Fats: **15 grams**
Carbohydrates: **35 grams**

Ingredients:

• Almond milk: 2 tablespoons
• Zucchini: 2 pieces
• Almond paste: 100 g
• Honey: 2 tablespoons
• Dates: 4 pieces
• Cinnamon: 1 teaspoon
• Ginger: 200 g

Cooking instructions:

1. Use a small beetroot.

2. Blend all the ingredients in a blender.

Notes

Banana-strawberry smoothie

- ◆ 2 servings
- ◆ 15 min
- ◆ 6 ingredients

Nutritional value per serving:

Calories: **799 kcal**

Proteins: **14 grams**

Fats: **40 grams**

Carbohydrates: **96 grams**

Ingredients:

- Iceberg lettuce: 200 g
- Coconut milk: 2 cups
- Bananas: 2 pieces
- Apples: 2 pieces
- Frozen strawberries: 2 cups
- Ground flaxseeds: 4 tablespoons

Cooking instructions:

1. Cut all the ingredients into cubes and add them to the blender.

2. Blend for 1–2 minutes until smooth.

Notes

Desserts

Low-calorie muffins

- ◆ 10 servings
- ◆ 40 min
- ◆ 8 ingredients

Nutritional value per serving:

Calories: **179 kcal**
Proteins: **6 grams**
Fats: **6 grams**
Carbohydrates: **26 grams**

Ingredients:

- Kefir: 1 cup
- Oat flakes: 2¼ cups
- Nuts: 67 g
- Raisins: 122 g
- Chicken eggs: 2¼ pieces
- Salt: a pinch
- Baking soda: ½ teaspoon
- Cinnamon: a pinch

Cooking instructions:

1. Soak whole flakes (1 cup) in kefir and let sit for 10 minutes. Grind the remaining cup of flakes.

2. Beat the eggs with salt, baking soda, and spices, then add to the flakes. Mix well.

3. While stirring, add the ground flakes, raisins, and nuts.

4. Pour the mixture into greased muffin molds. They can be metal, silicone, or paper.

5. Bake in the oven at 350 degrees for 20 minutes.

Notes

Low-calorie charlotte

◆ 4 servings
◆ 60 min
◆ 7 ingredients

Nutritional value per serving:

Calories: **169 kcal**
Proteins: **5 grams**
Fats: **2 grams**
Carbohydrates: **31 grams**

Ingredients:

- Flour: 50 g
- Chicken egg: 1 piece
- Apples: 2 pieces
- Baking powder: 1 teaspoon
- Sugar: 6 teaspoons
- Cinnamon: to taste
- Fat-free kefir: 200 ml

Cooking instructions:

1. Peel the apples, remove the cores, slice them, and arrange in a baking dish.

2. Beat the egg with sugar, add the kefir, sifted flour, and baking powder, and knead the dough.

3. Pour the batter over the apples and bake for 30–50 minutes at 360 degrees until golden brown.

Notes

Oatmeal cookies with cherries and zest

◆ 6 servings
◆ 20 min
◆ 10 ingredients

Nutritional value per serving:

Calories: **365 kcal**

Proteins: **11 grams**

Fats: **9 grams**

Carbohydrates: **60 grams**

Ingredients:

• Oat flakes: 2 cups
• Natural fat-free yogurt: 100 g
• Wheat flour: ½ cup
• Honey: 4 tablespoons
• Chicken eggs: 2 pieces

• Dried cherries: 150 g
• Almonds: 50 g
• Orange zest: 50 g
• Ground cinnamon: ⅓ teaspoon
• Rum: 30 ml

Cooking instructions:

1. Preheat the oven to 360 degrees. In a bowl, mix the yogurt, honey, eggs, flour, rum, and cinnamon using a mixer or blender.

2. Then add the oat flakes, chopped almonds, cherries, and zest.

3. Form the mixture into balls using a teaspoon and place them on baking paper, a couple of centimeters apart.

4. Bake for about 15 minutes, until the cookies are golden brown. Serve hot.

Notes

Low-calorie, sugar-free ice cream

- ◆ 4 servings
- ◆ 15 min
- ◆ 3 ingredients

Nutritional value per serving:

Calories: **29 kcal**
Proteins: **1 grams**
Fats: **1 grams**
Carbohydrates: **4 grams**

Ingredients:

- Natural fat-free yogurt: 150 g
- Fructose: 5 g
- Frozen blueberries: 150 g

Cooking instructions:

1. The berries should be frozen. Combine the yogurt and berries in a blender, and blend everything into a thick mixture. Add sweetener to taste. You can use any berries you like.

Notes

Low-calorie oatmeal pancakes with feta cheese

- ◆ 4 servings
- ◆ 15 min
- ◆ 7 ingredients

Nutritional value per serving:

Calories: **304 kcal**
Proteins: **12 grams**
Fats: **7 grams**
Carbohydrates: **50 grams**

Ingredients:

- Oat flakes: 2 cups
- Fat-free milk: 2 cups
- Wheat flour: 2 tablespoons
- Chicken eggs: 2 pieces
- Baking soda: 2 teaspoons
- Sugar: 2 teaspoons
- Feta cheese: to taste

Cooking instructions:

1. Mix 1 cup of oat flakes with 1/3 cup of milk (the milk should be at room temperature.

2. Beat the remaining milk with the egg (until frothy), then add the sugar and whisk.

3. Thoroughly blend the oat flakes with the milk, then add the milk beaten with eggs and sugar, one tablespoon of flour, and blend everything again. After that, add the baking soda. Let it sit for at least 40 minutes.

4. Then stir gently with a large spoon from the bottom up until smooth.

5. Fry on a preheated skillet (grease the skillet with oil the first time, and cook the rest without oil).

6. Fry until bubbles appear, then flip and cook for another 8–10 seconds.

7. Serve with feta cheese (or any other cheese or filling; feel free to add fruits).

Notes

Chocolate fondant made with dark chocolate

◆ 4 servings
◆ 30 min
◆ 7 ingredients

Nutritional value per serving:

Calories: **650 kcal**
Proteins: **16 grams**
Fats: **40 grams**
Carbohydrates: **57 grams**

Ingredients:

• Wheat flour: 20 g
• Chicken eggs: 4 pieces
• Sugar: 50 g
• Cocoa powder: 50 g

• Black coffee: 5 g
• Dark chocolate (70%): 300 g
• Butter: 20 g

Cooking instructions:

1. Place the chocolate in a double boiler and wait until it completely melts.

2. Mix the eggs, flour, and sugar (whisk until smooth.

3. Once the chocolate has melted, add the cocoa and butter while removing it from the double boiler, then pour in the mixture.

4. Pour the mixture into the molds in which you will be serving.

5. Bake at 450 degrees for 5 minutes for a molten center, or 7 minutes for a thicker center.

Notes

Low-calorie cottage cheese cheesecake

◆ 8 servings
◆ 90 min
◆ 10 ingredients

Nutritional value per serving:

Calories: **200 kcal**
Proteins: **19 grams**
Fats: **12 grams**
Carbohydrates: **4 grams**

Ingredients:

- Chicken eggs: 2 pieces
- Soft fat-free cottage cheese: 500 g
- Sour cream (10% fat): 200 g
- Sugar substitute: to taste
- Vanilla: a pinch
- Sorbitol: to taste
- Fiber: 100 g
- Apple juice: to taste
- Coconut flakes: to taste
- Ricotta cheese: 450 g

Cooking instructions:

1. Blend the cottage cheese, ricotta, and sour cream using blender or mixer. Dissolve the sugar substitute (stevia or stevia glycoside works best) in a teaspoon of lemon juice and add it to the cheese mixture. Taste for sweetness and adjust to your preference. It's best to use a combination of stevia glycoside and sorbitol, as using only stevia can result in an unpleasant taste.

2. Add the eggs, vanilla, and coconut flakes to the cheese mixture and blend quickly.

3. Take enough fiber to form the base for the cheesecake. Add apple juice to the fiber in a separate bowl until you achieve a mixture suitable for the crust. You can also add chopped nuts or dried fruits. Spread the mixture on the bottom of a springform pan, distribute, and press down firmly. Place in a preheated oven at 350 degrees and bake for 7–10 minutes.

4. Remove the pan with the crust from the oven and let it cool to room temperature.

5. Pour the cheese mixture over the crust. Gently shake the cheesecake pan several times to remove any excess air bubbles. Cover the top of the pan with foil. Ideally, place the cheesecake pan inside a larger pan filled with water, ensuring the water reaches halfway up the sides of the cheesecake pan. This is acceptable only if the cheesecake pan is entirely leak-proof. As a precaution, you can wrap the bottom of the cheesecake pan with foil to prevent water from getting in. Alternatively, you can place the cheesecake pan on the top shelf of the oven and put a heatproof dish filled with cold water one or two levels below it.

6. Bake for about 1 hour at 180 degrees. After an hour, check the cheesecake's readiness—the center should be slightly undercooked and wobble. Turn off the oven and let it cool inside for another hour. Remove from the oven and allow it to cool to room temperature, then transfer to the refrigerator. It's best to let it chill overnight.

Chocolate truffles with curry and mango

- ◆ 4 servings
- ◆ 30 min
- ◆ 5 ingredients

Nutritional value per serving:
Calories: **605 kcal**
Proteins: **7 grams**
Fats: **41 grams**
Carbohydrates: **50 grams**

Ingredients:

- Whipped cream: 1¼ cups
- Curry powder: 1 teaspoon
- Dark chocolate (70%): 260 g
- Mango: 1 piece
- Shredded coconut: to taste

Cooking instructions:

1. Peel the mango and blend it into a puree in a blender. You should get about 0.5 cups. Pour the cream into a saucepan and bring it to a boil, add the curry. Remove from heat and let it cool for 10 minutes, then add the mango puree. Mix well.

2. Meanwhile, melt 200 grams of chocolate in a double boiler. Remove from heat and add another 60 grams. Mix well and add the cream. Place in the refrigerator for about 3 hours until set.

3. Line a large plate with parchment paper. Take 2 teaspoons of the chocolate mixture and form balls. Place shredded coconut in a bowl and roll the truffles in it, gently pressing. Arrange on the prepared plate. Refrigerate for 1 hour.

Pineapple protein low-calorie ice cream

♦ 2 servings
♦ 30 min
♦ 4 ingredients

Nutritional value per serving:

Calories: **277 kcal**
Proteins: **40 grams**
Fats: **1 grams**
Carbohydrates: **26 grams**

Ingredients:

• Fat-free cottage cheese: 460 g

• Pineapple: 400 g

• Fat-free kefir: 100 ml

• Sugar substitute tablets: 10 tablets (adjust to taste)

Cooking instructions:

1. Remove the cottage cheese from the fridge. Any type will work including dry, crumbly types and creamy, spreadable ones. I used a crumbly variety.

2. If using crumbly, unsalted cottage cheese, press it through a fine sieve. Those using creamy, spreadable types can skip this step.

3. The pineapple or any other fruit filling should be frozen.

4. Take the fruit out of the freezer and let it thaw slightly to avoid needing a heavy-duty tool. While it sits, grate the cottage cheese.

5. Add kefir to the cottage cheese and blend it into a smooth, uniform mixture. The texture should become perfectly creamy.

6. Add the sugar substitute to the mixture.

7. Chop the pineapple or your chosen fruit— it should be slightly softened for cutting but not completely thawed.

8. Mix everything together, place it in the freezer for about 15 minutes. It's best to use a plastic container and spread the mixture along the sides — this will help it freeze faster.

Notes

Biscotti with hazelnuts

◆ 2 servings
◆ 60 min
◆ 5 ingredients

Nutritional value per serving:
Calories: **649 kcal**
Proteins: **15 grams**
Fats: **36 grams**
Carbohydrates: **38 grams**

Ingredients:

• Hazelnuts: 200 g
• Sugar: 100 g
• Chicken egg: 1 piece

• Wheat flour: 200 g
• Vanilla bean: 1 pod (or 1 teaspoon of vanilla extract)

Cooking instructions:

1. Toast the nuts in a dry skillet until they become fragrant, and their skins peel off. Remove the skins, transfer the nuts to a blender, add sugar, and blend until smooth.

2. Transfer the mixture to a mixer, add the sifted flour, the contents of the vanilla pod, and the egg, and mix until you have a firm dough. Mix until you have a firm dough. Roll out thin sausages, place them on a baking sheet, and bake in the oven for 25 minutes.

3. While they are still hot, cut the sausages and let them cool down in that shape.

Notes

Puff pastry cookies with parmesan

◆ 12 servings
◆ 25 min
◆ 3 ingredients

Nutritional value per serving:

Calories: **109 kcal**
Proteins: **4 grams**
Fats: **7 grams**
Carbohydrates: **6 grams**

Ingredients:

• Unleavened puff pastry: 200 g
• Egg: 1 piece

• Parmesan cheese: 100 g

Cooking instructions:

1. Prepare all the ingredients. Preheat the oven to 360 degrees.

2. Take the dough out of the freezer.

3. Roll out the dough to a thickness of about 2 mm.

4. Prick the dough all over with a fork.

5. Lightly beat the egg.

6. Brush the dough with the beaten egg using a pastry brush.

7. Sprinkle the dough with grated Parmesan cheese.

8. Use cookie cutters to cut out shapes from the dough.

9. Transfer the cookies to a baking sheet lined with parchment paper. Bake for 10–15 minutes. Let the finished cookies cool on a wire rack.

Notes

Berry-fruit no-bake dessert

- ◆ 8 servings
- ◆ 30 min
- ◆ 7 ingredients

Nutritional value per serving:

Calories: **310 kcal**
Proteins: **6 grams**
Fats: **14 grams**
Carbohydrates: **41 grams**

Ingredients:

- Butter: 60 g
- Cookies: 150 g
- Gelatin: 1 tablespoon
- Strawberry yogurt: 500 g
- Sugar: ½ cup
- Frozen berries: 500 g
- Cream: 200 g

Cooking instructions:

1. Crush the cookies in a blender into crumbs and mix with butter. Then transfer the resulting dough into a mold (we use one with a diameter of 22 cm), flatten it out, and put it in the refrigerator.

2. Thaw the berries and drain the juice. Dissolve the gelatin in the juice, let it swell for 30–40 minutes, and then heat it until fully dissolved (do not bring it to a boil!

3. Add sugar to the berries, blend them lightly, mix with the yogurt, then add the gelatin. Wait until it sets a little, then pour it into the mold with the base.

4. Let it set in the refrigerator.

5. For a more festive version, whip 200 ml of heavy cream (at least 30%) and add it to the soufflé after the gelatin. The flavor will become even creamier.

Notes

Almond truffles with cinnamon

◆ 4 servings
◆ 15 min
◆ 6 ingredients

Nutritional value per serving:

Calories: **757 kcal**
Proteins: **19 grams**
Fats: **49 grams**
Carbohydrates: **66 grams**

Ingredients:

- Almonds: 333 g
- Ground cinnamon: 2¾ tablespoons
- Raisins: 227 g
- Honey: 6¾ tablespoons
- Olive oil: 1¼ tablespoons
- Salt: to taste

Cooking instructions:

1. Blend the almonds (or substitute with walnuts) until finely chopped. Add cinnamon and a pinch of salt, and mix well. Rinse the raisins and remove any stems. Combine them in a bowl with the nuts, then pour in honey or agave nectar and olive oil. Optionally, you can add a touch of vanilla and nutmeg to enhance the flavor.

2. Roll the mixture into balls or logs and coat with coconut flakes.

Notes

Chocolate truffles with lemon and thyme

◆ 4 servings
◆ 30 min
◆ 7 ingredients

Nutritional value per serving:

Calories: **554 kcal**
Proteins: **7 grams**
Fats: **41 grams**
Carbohydrates: **42 grams**

Ingredients:

• Whipped cream: 1¼ cups
• 70% dark chocolate: 260 g
• Fresh thyme: 1½ teaspoons

• Lemon juice: 1½ tablespoons
• Lemon zest: 1 teaspoon
• Cocoa powder: to taste

Cooking instructions:

1. Pour the cream into a saucepan and bring it to a boil, adding finely chopped thyme. Remove from heat and let it cool for 20 minutes. Then add the lemon juice and grated lemon zest. Mix well.

2. Meanwhile, melt 200 grams of chocolate in a double boiler. Remove from heat and add another 60 grams. Mix well and add the cream. Place in the refrigerator for about 3 hours until set.

Notes

Crème brulé with liqueur

◆ 4 servings
◆ 60 min
◆ 4 ingredients

Nutritional value per serving:

Calories: **269 kcal**
Proteins: **4 grams**
Fats: **23 grams**
Carbohydrates: **11 grams**

Ingredients:

• Egg yolks: 4
• Heavy cream (33%): 225 ml

• Sugar: 35 g
• Vanilla: to taste

Cooking instructions:

1. Mix the egg yolks with the sugar.

2. Heat the cream with the vanilla until it reaches a boil. Then, strain it into the egg yolks while stirring vigorously to prevent them from curdling. Add 2 teaspoons of Baileys.

3. Pour the mixture into molds and place them in the oven at 260 degrees to bake. The time will depend on the size of your containers, typically around 20–25 minutes. Let cool before serving.

Notes

Dessert with pumpkin, cranberries, and dried apricots

- ◆ 4 servings
- ◆ 60 min
- ◆ 8 ingredients

Nutritional value per serving:

Calories: **195 kcal**
Proteins: **3 grams**
Fats: **12 grams**
Carbohydrates: **21 grams**

Ingredients:

- Butternut squash (or any squash): 500 g
- Extra virgin olive oil: 2 tablespoon
- Apple cider vinegar: 1 tablespoon
- Salt: ¼ teaspoon
- Freshly ground black pepper: ¼ teaspoon
- Dried apricots (chopped): 40 g
- Dried cranberries: 40 g
- Toasted almond flakes: 2 tablespoons

Cooking instructions:

1. Cut the squash lengthwise into 4 pieces, remove the seeds, and slice it crosswise into skinny slices.

2. Steam the squash until soft for 5–7 minutes. Mix the vinegar, salt, pepper, and olive oil in a large bowl. Add the squash, finely chopped dried apricots, and cranberries. Toss to combine, sprinkle with nuts, and serve.

Notes

Semifreddo with pistachios and balsamic cream

- ◆ 4 servings
- ◆ 300 min
- ◆ 6 ingredients

Nutritional value per serving:

Calories: **532 kcal**
Proteins: **16 grams**
Fats: **45 grams**
Carbohydrates: **16 grams**

Ingredients:

- Unsalted pistachios: 200 g
- Pistachio paste: 200 g
- Heavy cream (35%): 400 ml
- Sugar: 5 tablespoons
- Egg whites: 4
- Balsamic cream: to taste

Cooking instructions:

1. Peel the pistachios and blend them in a blender or chop them with a knife into a medium crumb. Whip room temperature egg whites with a pinch of salt until firm peaks form, then gradually add the sugar one tablespoon at a time, beating until glossy and stable peaks form. The egg whites are perfectly whipped if they hold their shape and do not fall when you turn the bowl upside down.

2. Whip the cold liquid cream in a separate bowl until it becomes thick and fluffy. Like the egg whites, the cream is perfectly whipped if it holds its shape and does not fall when you turn the bowl upside down.

3. Combine the whipped cream with the pistachio paste and chopped pistachios, gently folding from the bottom up in several additions to avoid deflating the whipped structure of the cream. Gently incorporate this mixture with the whipped egg whites with the same care and method. The result will be a smooth pistachio cream in a light khaki color.

4. Pour the cream into a loaf pan lined with plastic wrap. The wrap should completely cover the bottom and hang over the edges of the pan. Cover the semifreddo with another wrap, pinching the top and bottom edges together. Place it in the freezer for 4 hours until set.

5. Slice the semifreddo with a knife into portions and serve with a generous drizzle of balsamic cream.

Apple soufflé

◆ 4 servings
◆ 60 min
◆ 4 ingredients

Nutritional value per serving:
Calories: **204 kcal**
Proteins: **4 grams**
Fats: **1 grams**
Carbohydrates: **43 grams**

Ingredients:

• Red apples: 5 pieces
• Sugar: 67 g

• Lemon zest: to taste
• Gelatin: 1¼ teaspoons (13 g)

Cooking instructions:

1. Wash and peel the apples. Then, remove the cores and seeds. Cut into small pieces.

2. Add sugar and simmer covered without adding water over low heat.

3. Grate the lemon zest. Add the zest to the nearly cooked apples.

4. Mix everything and continue to cook until done.

5. Puree the apple mixture with a blender.

6. Prepare the gelatin according to the instructions on the package and stir it into the apple puree. Whip the mixture until it starts to turn white. Whip until the desired consistency is achieved (about 5 minutes should be enough).

7. Divide into containers and refrigerate if desired to set.

8. Garnish and serve.

Notes

Vegetarian cranberry no-bake cake

◆ 4 servings
◆ 480 min
◆ 13 ingredients

Nutritional value per serving:

Calories: **505 kcal**
Proteins: **25 grams**
Fats: **94 grams**
Carbohydrates: **48 grams**

Ingredients:

• Cranberries: 500g
• Chia seeds: 1½ teaspoons
• Honey: 5 tablespoons
• Cashews: 500 g

• Lemon juice: ½ cup
• Vanilla extract: 1 teaspoon
• Lemon zest: 1 piece
• Salt: a pinch

Cooking instructions:

1. For a 24 cm diameter mold, line the bottom of a springform pan with high sides (about 5 cm) with a circle of parchment paper. This is a precaution, but it makes it easier to remove the cake.

2. Mix one cup of lingonberries, chia seeds, and 2 teaspoons of honey for the jam, and let it sit until it thickens. Then add 1-1.5 teaspoons of pectin and stir well.

3. For the cream, blend all the remaining lingonberries (previously puréed), cashews (soaked in cold water for 8-10 hours), lemon juice, honey, vanilla extract, and lemon zest in a food processor until very smooth. Then add the coconut oil and mix well.

4. Spread half of the mixture over the base, add a few spoonsful of the jam on top. Then add the second half of the berry mixture. Add the remaining jam and create a pattern. Place in the refrigerator for 8-12 hours.

Notes

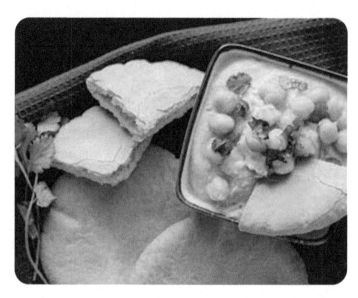

Pita flatbread

- ◆ 4 servings
- ◆ 180 min
- ◆ 7 ingredients

Nutritional value per serving:

Calories: **248 kcal**
Proteins: **6 grams**
Fats: **3 grams**
Carbohydrates: **49 grams**

Ingredients:

- Unbleached wheat flour: 58 g
- Wheat flour: 192 g
- Salt: to taste
- Sugar: 1 teaspoon
- Water: 225 ml
- Olive oil: 1 teaspoon
- Dry yeast: 4 g

Cooking instructions:

1. Mix the flour and add sugar, salt, and yeast. While stirring constantly, pour in the water and olive oil.

2. Cover the dough and let it rise in a warm place for 1 hour.

3. Punch down the dough and divide it into 6 equal parts. Roll each part out thinly, place them on foil brushed with olive oil. Let them rise for 1 hour.

4. Preheat the oven to 260°C (500°F). Bake the pitas for 5-6 minutes.

Notes

Notes

Tips for Achieving Maximum Results on the Mediterranean Diet

1. Drink 2 glasses of water with lemon after waking up to kick-start your digestive system.

2. Have 3-4 meals a day with intervals of 3-4 hours.

3. Have your last meal at 6-7 PM.

4. Avoid snacking.

5. Drink water and other beverages 30 minutes before or after meals.

6. Take at least 5,000 steps per day.

7. Do 3 workouts per week.

Made in the USA
Las Vegas, NV
14 December 2024

14258599R00098